Elton D. Jones
To Break Free: Quarantine

Published by: Jones Publishing LLC

Text Design by: Elton D. Jones

Cover Design by: Elton D. Jones

A CIP record for this book is available from the Library of
Congress Cataloging-in-Publication Data

ISBN-13: 978-0-9836783-3-5

Distributed by:

Ingram Content Group
1 Ingram Blvd
La Vergne, TN, 37086
Printed and bound in Location by Lightning Source Inc.

1

Elton D. Jones
TO BREAK FREE: QUARANTINE

REVIEWS

About The Author

Find a troubled soul, looking to still find triumphs in a dark time:

When we fall down hard, how many of us can perform CPR?

A way to bring the self back to life.

Man I fell hard! Took a lot of people down too;

They tried to catch me. Hearts broken down hard.

Euphorically broken bones, bruises and scratches,

Can leave a long trail of physical pain;

Ice cold human interactions!

Must be intentional on our daily interactions.

Grateful for each and every passing day.

Only given this won moment to be here in the now.

How many will make this second your shining best?

Even when the fleeting moments seem grey and dull?

For no one is promised tomorrow!

Gotta do what we gotta do today.

When all else will take the similar route,

I dare to go the narrow way.

To Break Free:

A collection from 2009 Ingham County Jail/Mason MI

added with the collection created in 2010, the first 40 day entrance to the

Michigan Department of Corruptions.

QUARANTINE

Thank you

For The Strength to Never Quit

To Break Free:

QUARANTINE

by Elton D. Jones

CONTENTS

HAPPYNESS DEPENDS ON OURSELVES.

TO BREAK FREE:

THE POSITIVE THINKER SEES THE INVISIBLE, FEELS THE INTANGIBLE, AND ACHIEVES THE IMPOSSIBLE.

THE CHOICE TO BE EXCELLENT BEGINS WITH ALIGNING YOUR THOUGHTS AND WORDS WITH THE INTENTION TO REQUIRE MORE FROM YOURSELF.

PERPETUAL OPTIMISM IS A FORCE MULTIPLIER.

CHOOSE THE POSITIVE. YOU HAVE A CHOICE. YOU ARE THE MASTER OF YOUR ATTITUDE. CHOOSE THE POSITIVE, THE CONSTRUCTIVE.

OPTIMISM IS THE MOST IMPORTANT HUMAN TRAIT BECAUSE IT ALLOWS US TO EVOLVE OUR IDEAS, TO IMPROVE OUR SITUATION, AND TO HOPE FOR A BETTER TOMORROW.

ALL THAT WE ARE IS THE RESULT OF WHAT WE HAVE THOUGHT. THE MIND IS EVERYTHING. WE THINK, WE BECOME.

BUDDHA

TO ACCOMPLISH HER PURPOSE

Find me broken,
So far away from my perfect self:
Frustrated and angry;
Not quite at 100% mental health;
Locked away in jail!
Is this time spent in prison the true definition of me?

A hoe out on the street;
A prostitute my occupation,
Out here just trying to make a living in these tough streets
I Am everyday facing!
When God has a need to fill
Is it true that She can use me?
Competent with the gang of misfits;!
The disciples completed work way beyond belief.
So far from complete, not quite yet made whole.
My God will still use you
To chart glory for the whole!
I am an example!
If He can do this through me…….
So much to be grateful for;
He chose to use me.
Ridiculed and lowly,
Accident prone and mistake-filled is me!
Bandages on my elbows,
Cuts and scrapes on my hands and knees!
Hoist by my own petard
Maginot Line no more!
My sense of security has been knocked down
Leaving me high strung no more.
Exposed and vulnerable!
Moldable to do His Will.
If you will but use me Lord
Whatever you say, I will.

SOMETHING TO PRAY FOR

"And ye became followers of us, and of the Lord, having received the word in much affliction, with joy of the Holy Ghost." 1 Thessalonians 1:6

Find me in the midst of this adversity!
Don't know exactly why or how such troubles has come:
This lump on the breast; Pain of chest!
They can't figure out from whence this mass in the brain has cum!
Give me the reason!
When is it that we pray our best:
A loved one gone to prison;
No longer due to have the comfort of my child upon my chest!
Who will protect my seed?
While it is that I am away?
Where is the angel of protection that will keep Mom's mind strong?
And from Dad, to take the drugs away!
How many will rest in the midst of the storm!
In the midst of my ill-comfort zone can I sleep?
Is this thing of urgency enough for me to just be at peace?
If there is no confusion, will you so choose to put your spiritual warrior to test!
How much time on knees will be spent,
Before all of the hurt has been lain to rest?
Praying without ceasing, when these troubles come my way!
Who needs a reason?
To fulfill the reason of why She so often went to the garden anyway.
Thank you God when it's all positive;
All of these dark clouds taken away!
Don't even care who's looking,
Need to kneel down before the cross for today;
Take this time out to pray!
Who is there that will calm the tears down?
Send light unto the lost!
Come find this sheep Lord,
Sorry that I got lost!
If only I could touch the hem of His sleeve!
All of this would just dissipate.
Go away and go right now,
Back to the way it was before all of the hate.
Before all of these troubles came about,
Confusion has cum my way.
Not now is this the ending to this
Have to live on just one more day,
Get through to the meaning of all of this

12

INNER TREASURE

"If I say, surely the darkness shall cover me; even the night shall be light about me. Yea, the darkness hideth not from thee; but the night shineth as the day! The darkness and the light are both alike to thee."

Psalm 139:11-12

Where is it that you focus?
On what does your mind's eye see?
Swaddling cloth and stench! Although he is a King!
Ordered to come in this way, no matter which it may be.
Living here in this pig pen,
And still She knows exactly where I be.
How many will judge on appearance;
Only focused on what we see.
Not attuned enough to the spirit,
To see what's going on deep down on the inside of me!
It's not the temple that's important, but what's on the inside is key.
Why do you wash the outside of the cup,
And leave it filthy from whence you drink?
Look to those around you,
Deep down what do you see?
The ego would love to see darkness,
And not the spirit-filled light that lives deep down inside of me.
What is important?
Does the myrrh, frankincense, and gold define thee?
Blinded by the gifts
When the true light lies deep down inside of me.
How do we move beyond? Get far away from all of the stink?
Get through the garments, these names can't define me.
Eating from this thing,
Food that you know not of,
How many have been filled by manna?
Not knowing it's reigning down from God up above.
Food falling from above!
Not content with the good,
We being so used to the bad!
Even here I can hold my head up to good
Knowing that this wilderness is just a place to be passed!
Through many dangers!
I'm on my way!
Just got to keep on moving,
Walk on for just one more day.

13

JUST 1 RAY

Trying to get to the big picture,
Not sure of the correct way!
I promise that you can get there,
If you find just one single ray.
Following each ray to goodness;
Finding the correct way.
Why choose to do good
Even in such a dark place!
Finding joy.
In such an unjoyful space.
It all begins with just one event; One single, small, little ray.

Giving my last to one
That I may not even be on the best of terms with.
Being thankful anyway,
Even for something that I may not have asked to get!
Needing to see the reason,
Being led to the correct door.
Searching my way back to you,
Following each and every opening,
Through which is the lit door!
Only to touch the hem of His garment
And watch it all go away.
Won't even need the whole thing,
Begin with just a small mustard seed of faith!
Tomorrow, for me, isn't promised,
But I will practice good intent toward men for today.

FAILURE

Tell me what is the reason?
That your thing did not happen!
Giving the devil the credit for this
When it's by God that you must endure this disaster!
Closing doors,
And allowing there to be lack!
For an intended purpose!
It was important for you to go through that.
Who can continue to praise?
When all the carnal mind sees is hell?
Ask Hannah why it took so long!
Ask Jesus why He had to go through hell.
To Abraham was given the promise
Well, I am the promise fulfilled!
How long has he been gone?
How long has he been outta here!
Who gleaned behind the reaper?
And for her was left more than enough!
For what was the reason?
Was there such an issue of blood?
Find the spirit at work,
In the mood to teach!
If we could just control the ego's feud;
Wipe this pride up off of me!
Praising Him anyway! Although this time did not go my way!
You call it failure!
I know this as going a different way.
All was not yet ready
Preparing me for a specific time, and this particular place.
Not sure of your understanding,
But me and my house will steadily praise Her name.
Continuing to check each and every one;
For me I know that She has opened up Her hands!
How will I complain being Her son?
Knowing that it's only God's will that has allowed me to keep moving on.
For me the thing was unnecessary,
Not needed for the growth of me.
The importance of failure!
Needed for the creation of me.

Thankful for this failure.
Grateful for this thing of death
That you used to bring life onto me.
None of the old me left!
Allowed this thing to be birthed through me,
Now I know this child ain't mine!
Pushed into my purpose
So the blessing I give back onto the divine!
When all thought that this was over,
You made all things anew!
Knowing this wasn't over.
Knew we'd make it through.
In the mean time, just keep on rolling,
Using the failures to make all things new.
Either we learning or we growing,
But never is it curtains closed when with you.
Just not through,
Failure's not an option,
Will only keep rolling forward
Failure can't stop us.

TOO CLOSE

Came this far!
How do we dare turn back now?
Military crawl, limp, or walk;
Just got to get there
The best way that we know how!
Thought the light was closer
Seeing the flicker now for so many traveled miles!
Just have to keep on moving,
Far too close to give up on the goal now!
Too tired to run,
Anxious to be right there right now.
Guided by this flickering light,
Just gotta get there,
Somehow!
Tired and thirsty,
Yet too focused to eat
Looking to find some small comforts;
Get these wet shoes off of my feet!
Continuing to praise!
Though those wet garments are so heavy!
Just when it felt that I was right there
The cold began to blow even more heavy.

THERE ARE NO GREAT LIMITS TO GROWTH BECAUSE

THERE ARE NO LIMITS OF HUMAN INTELLIGENCE,

IMAGINATION, AND WONDER.
RONALD REAGAN

BORN ON THA HIT LIST

A glorious day in the heavens,
To equal out to an ugly one here on earth!
Judge me by where I am;
Because of my destiny, I am plucked out from the earth.
In a world where the outside world cannot even see!
The prince of darkness already knows,
Born in this barn for a reason,
Wrapped in this swaddling cloth, out on the street in the cold!
Remember Moses?
Hidden right where the Egyptians everyday would see.
Christ treated the same way,
Came here to dwell with man, not to blasphemy.
Had to learn of this way.
Had to live the way of man so now we can follow em back.
See David in the mountains,
Paul put away by thoughts of man!
Though we can't see the reason, in heaven it's a gloriously unfolded plan!
The angels are singing
As the Holy Spirit leads the way.
Put in a dark place for safety;
Protected for your perfect day.
Why God came in this likeness?
To fulfill the deal of this thing.
You are not this body!
The spirit man is the real thing.
Holy in the spiritual,
The carnal does not feel a thing.
Born on the hit list,
No matter what I do, they'll still be judging me!
Not of this world,
So how is it that you could ever mold me?
Brought here to be peculiar!
I am unique in this ring.
Who would ever understand?
If He did come as the king!
He has already been through this
Why would I expect you to do right by me?

Been on this hit list!
Long before the world ever bore me.
Tried to take me out early,
And by the grace of God I still breathe.
How many attempts have you had?
So many tries to take the life out of me!
By His angels, I'm still here.
Even in death will only find life in me!
Welcomed my awakening
Don't worry, She only sleeps!
Open up thy mind,
Finally enlightenment came into me;
Like Lazarus, He has called forth the best out of me.
Bound and chained,
Entangled by this tangled web we weave!
Tripped up by my own sin again,
Got this target set out on the back of me.
We already won!
Play your hand accordingly.
Born on the hit list!
But untouchable by God's authority.

HARRIET TUBMAN

"Then Jesus, looking at him, loved him, and said to him, 'One thing you lack:
go your way, sell whatever you have and give to the poor, and you will have
treasure in heaven: and come, take up the cross, and follow me."
Mark 10:21

See me as a modern day train conductor,
Carrying this world to its best.
No longer moving by the North Star,
But it's the Holy Spirit that will lead us to this rest.
Where is your investment?
Shed light on this gloomy world
This is all a matter of perception,
Where is your vision of the world?
If time is not real;
Not engineered by God.
If sin is but an illusion,
Then how much of life, by death
Have we been robbed?
Decided to sell all
To make an investment in something much greater!
How will I feel love?
If without you I go back to the maker.
If He was born to lead,
And through Him I live too.
Once I've found the secret,
Like Her, I must also guide you!
Following the rays,
Making our way back to The Teacher!
The tracks are no longer underground;
Available to all of the seekers.
Those who ask, it shall be given.
The ones who seek are promised to find.
It's the Kingdom of heaven that we're looking for
And it's lying dormant within our mind's!
Where is your treasure?
Where do you hold what's dear to you?
The will is the one true currency we hold;
To life or death is more important than riches to you?
Making my investment
In this belief of life!
Sold all of my stock in death,
And then doubled down on life.

SHE WILL FIND ME

How big is my problem?
Large enough for me to lose hope?
Been faithful for so long
What's the reason to keep on moving in this hope?
Steadily believing and believing
In this thing I know that She knows!
With just a touch of Her skirt,
I know that She will heal all of my woes!
Believing that I am important;
Deserving of His personal being!
Because I am a Child of God
I know that She won't leave me here.

THIS FOUNDATION

You may keep on laughing,
At my current impediment that you see.
I know exactly what I'm doing;
Perfect soil is what I need.
So out of this, will make the best of me;
Find me out here digging!
Burrowing deep down into the soul of me, looking to find the meaning.
Need to build where it's sturdiest!
Searching for the destined rock, solid, and sturdy that's underneath
From there, my build can proceed!
No matter the impediments, or the soil type,
If I just dig down far enough is all I need!
I will find the type of rock, that is just right for me;
Perfect for the growth of us!
Lost in the preparation,
For this perfect plan that must be.
You may not believe it now,
But I've got the blood of Noah inside of me.
Given this vision,
A future thing that must be.
Right now just gotta keep digging
Until the rock presents itself unto me.

THE PRINCIPLE

Who is there that will help me?
In the midst of this mighty storm!
Yes, I know it's the Sabbath!
How long have I wished I could just move this thing along?
Fell in this hole today. Didn't do it on purpose,
Withered is my understanding
Limited is my perception of this Super Holy Person.
Just because it is this day
Is it true that I should be robbed!
Tell me what's more important;
The lesson? Or the student for which the lesson was brought?
If your cow should Fall into this hole……..
Now however could you leave a human behind!
How much do colors separate?
Or does my fall make yours feel better than mine?
Tell me about your heart.
Ability to fulfill a need.
Dare to hold me down!
Only to prove that you're better than me.
Not afraid to come down, to give help to a broken man!
How many will dare to lift his brother up?
Who is there that will give her a helping hand?

TO NOT LOSE SIGHT

Won't be misguided by current perception,
Led by this particular space and place in time.
Living life by something much bigger;
This vision imprinted in my mind.
Choose not to fall prey to these seconds,
Chose these minutes created by my mind.
Each hour that passes by is but a blessing!
How will one day decide the rest of your life?
If time is not real,
Where did the loss of these years go?
Too determined to live in the past
Must chose to look on to where we're planning to go.
In my current predicament! All may not look fine,
Must decide to keep on living,
And give the spiritual man a try.

ONCE ALL HOPE IS GONE!

Why is it that once we give up?
This thing that we've been waiting for finally comes to pass!
From patiently to anxiously,
Waiting until all of the time has past.
Still sitting and waiting, even when time seems to be of
Importance no more.
This thing that we were sure would be;
No longer are we now so certain for.
Now what am I to do?
When my sure thing moves right on past?
Well beyond the breaking point,
Darkness in every direction the eye is to pass.
Tell me why has this happened Lord?
Woe is me!
Crushed of all my strength,
Power drained right up out of me.
How do we still have faith?
When so much has happened along the way?
Wanting to see the destination,
When the promise was only held to
Those who kept on by faith.
Appointed to this certain position,
From this, however will it be?
Family decided to quit,
To let it all just be.
All of this gone against my will.
How to get His will to shine from the deep?
Too thirsty to walk,
And too hungry to read.
Waiting for some substance,
But who is out there that will feed me?
Will B;
In comparison to who I Am Right now?
Well bye bye to me.
No longer the me that you used to see,
Or even the me that you currently see.

Won't be held back by fear
Will only allow it to develop me.
Not held back by what I Am right now
I'm focused on who I plan to be.
Not afraid of failure.
Won't back down to success.
Called and appointed to a position
How many will stand up to the test?
Held back at the thought of perfection
This purpose calls forth for your personal best.
Tripped and fell down;
Still refused to settle for anything less!
With only a minute left for time,
The spirit still has so much time left.
Must work within the self
To remove this other voice that continues to speak of lack and less!
Sit down the ego!
With the Holy Spirit, must decide to count each blessing!
Still know that I Am a king!
Though I sit here doing this time!
Knowing my time in the belly of the fish
Won't stop my appointment with the Allmighty.
Fell down hard,
But still refused to die.
Decided to endure,
Even when it felt like my soul would cry!
Through all of the wails, just continued to believe,
Warring in the mind, until I find Christ deep within me..
Lost in this quarantine,
Still willing to fight for my life.
This life is stlll worth caring for,
Although in hell I currently reside.

ON MY WAY

Headed into my destiny!
From birth heralded this perfect place.
In order to get there,
What first is there that God had to fillet?
Trimming something back.
Making the heart feel lean.
By God I'll tell ya!
How much it hurt when all was taken away from me.
Worked so hard to get the stuff! All of the toys that I had.
Even the ones I call family,
Taken away from my grasp. If loosing is only a sign
That something better is to cum!......
Thought I could do this all by myself,
But couldn't see what was all wrong!
In order to reach this blessing,
What had to be pulled away?
Doesn't mean that I didn't love it.
Will come back at a later date.
The old blessing had to stop
So that this new thing could be.
What am I to do Lord?
When my accomplishments have begun to outgrow me!
Not afraid of where I was,
Nor comfortable where I currently be.
Must outgrow this comfort zone;
Not let the fear get the best of me.

"But put forth thine hand now, and touch all that he hath, and he will curse thee to thy face." Job 1:11

ONCE YOU WAKE UP, AND SMELL THE COFFEE,
IT'S HARD TO GO BACK TO SLEEP.

FRAN DRESCHER

WHEN I CLOSE MY EYES

So many here against me.
Tell me again what exactly have I done?
Share with me your misery;
The reason why, againt me, so many have cum.
Find me alone, or in the company of Won.
Why like this have you come against me?
I am your only begotten son!
Who is there to save me?
To whom can I run?
No this thing won't change me;
In me, His work has only just begun!
When I sit to close my eyes
To find out what it is that I see.
Witness this army of Her legion,
All here to protect me.
Just know that what will be will be,
Is so long ago already done.
Came here for a specific reason;
No I won't even run.
My time to serve my purpose,
Whatever it may be.
God I am here to serve you!
Whatever it is that you may need.

WHERE DOES YOUR STRENGTH LIE?

What is it that's being fought for?
Where does the war truly begin?
No he doesn't need your car.
Nor your house,
Not even your family and friends.
Master of deception!
Out to take control of your mind.
Knowing what you hold dear and close
he will shake to see what he finds!
What is the war truly for?
All of the fighting is over you!
Where does your peace of mind lie?
How easy is it for the atmosphere to overwhelm you?
Knowing who we are,
And what we came here to be!
satan do as you want
The world's peace does not define me!
I joy in hardships.
Praise over the troubles you bring.
In the midst of such a storm,
To sit here and smile, and still be at peace.
Not by you will I be shaken.
My mind has been defined by the King
He left me with this;
A crazy ability for my mind to be at peace!

THE FUEL

Tell me about your problems,
And exclaim, 'Why me.'
So many things I've been through,
Not set for the true purpose of me!
Reaching for my destiny, ever so much closer to my dreams.
Wondering how to get there,
How to just be finished with this wicked thing!
Moving through this process,
That leads me to what I Am destined to be!
Stumbling into my opportunity,
Not knowing this is exactly where my transition leads.
In order to get over that,
You first must go through this.
Who is willing to be humbled?
And still praise God through all of this!
Entering these gates with thanksgiving!
How many are happy during the ride!
Praising during the scary parts!
Still rejoicing even when we're lost during the ride!
Who would believe by being this,
You were only getting me ready to be that!
Sharpening the end,
Not even knowing this was getting us ready for the enemy's next attack!
Every day to find the self-doing this
Pushing the comfort zone until it no longer exists.
How many see my giant as impossible!
Well for me, just a chance to keep on growing through this.
While all else are ready to quit
Will you bring solely your courage to the fight?
The faith to keep on going,
When all else thought this was goodnight!
Entering the gates with thanksgiving!
Ready to just go out and handle it.
Tell me the outcome!
If we didn't have to keep battling to advance through this.
All of these failures
Are exactly what has brought me to you.

Stepped into the dilemma
And by it,
This dream has become true!
How else to find my blessing?
If first I did not have to go through you.
With Goliath standing at the gate,
Will you still decide to charge on through?
Thinking in your head,
'This fight is not for you'
Just gotta keep trying.
This next obstacle just gotta blow through!

TENACITY

Who is there that won't give up?
No matter how crazy this here may seem.
Lost my career. My house, my wife and my kids!
Still I decided to keep fighting through this thing.
Through this, to stand up!
No matter how hard, to you, this may seem!
Lights off, no food in the belly,
No money to pay the rent or heat!
How many failures can this one thing bring?
Tell me about the times this didn't work?
And still we wouldn't quit!
That which may make some question,
Has only brought so much strength through the conception of it!
The wheat with the tare!
Growing here side by side until done!
This thing here is called fate; It has to be done!
Who is there that can find joy,
When so much is so hectic in your space?
Must fight on until the end of this!
Won't give up
No matter how many obstacles in front of me you may place.

Who is willing to go through!
To be exactly where you need to be?
Haven't seen all of the wars,
Just want to be in the seat of the king!
How many are willing to do battle
In order to win the war?
Through the floods and deserts,
Before reaching that final door.
Take this cup of suffering away from me!
According to your will not mine.
What is it that one must go through?
This thing that you have suffered through time!
Your word says we will endure
And that we will win with time.
Able to step up to the challenge,
And turn the adversity into an opportunity of mine.
Didn't want to go through the situation
Only God knew the growth that would come.
So much battling going on in my mind
When all I had to do was speak the victory
For the battle to have already been won.

IN THE MIDST OF THE STORM

Reign clouds, and dark skies,
Looking into the eye of death.
Hoping for the rain and wind.
Quietness reminds me too much of death.
Made it to the eye of this thing!
Is it here that we will find peace?
How many will come out from hiding?
Not exactly sure of what this really means.
How do we survive this?
And how many will never have to go through?
Alarm systems, storm shutters, or dogs for security for you!
Thank God that the Angels are here,
And watching over you!
How bad that this thing could be
Waiting for the good to shine through!
To clean up and keep on passing through the streets!
Nothing more that we can do.
Who can remove the ill feelings?
How to make me again feel safe and whole with you.
Even when I Am not physically able to be,
What price for assurance, are we willing to pay?
To get back to nil
Back to what's been taken away;
Stripped and pulled away.
In the midst of this storm,
What exactly is it that your mind's eye sees?
What's your ability to make it through the storm?
Find your reason to believe.
Hold on to it for dear life,
We're just passing through the eye.
Get ready for round two,

A STAR IS BORN

Find me in a massive collision,
Or in an isolation that is all convoluted.
Bring me a coiled spring;
I'll show you exactly what to do with it!
Who had to go through this?
In order to be where you are right now.
If only I may flicker for 15 seconds,
In preparation for that short moment, I will continue to spar!
Shinning bright for the world to see.
No matter from where it is that you are!
A grand sight to behold
Before death again turns my light into dark!
Extraordinarily bizarre!
When you judge me by my past,
Or simply remember me, by what you seen of me last;
From my humble beginnings, until my troubled past!
The totality of this flash is me!
How many wrote me off as all bad?
Thinking this bloom was taking too long!
Turning out to be the perfect storm;
Not too short,
Nor too long for such an implosion to cum.
Watch this great flash of glory
And read back up on what comprises my life!
The total imprint of my destiny
The complete make-up is what makes me free!
Confined in such a small space
Enveloped by all of this heat.
Just wait for me to blast off
To end up where She needs me to be.
Put on your dark shades.
My explosion won't allow you to look directly at me

SOMETHING HAPPENED

On the road to Damascus
How many have been knocked off of the beast!
On the way to persecute some Christians
Until Jesus came about me.
Blinding the eyes, and filling the insides with light.
On the way to do injustice,
And out of it He made me right!
How many would believe?
That after my troubled past I've changed.
No longer excited by what I used to be,
Now I'm a whole new man!
Check the background;
Research me on Google!
And now look at the fruit that I have,
Ask me how'd you do this?
I know that I'm now my best man;
Taken on a whole new task in life.
What power is there to force such change?
Bring such a grand scale turnabout!
Bring such a transformation, and make new light!
Thought it was a bad thing,
But it took that to recreate this life!
No more of who I was, and not yet who I Am gonna be,
Just know that I've been changed
This new energy flows about inside of me.
From working to kill yall
To saving those that will follow me!
The Ones who Didn't..........
How many have you known?
Who said with you they will always be!
Then find you in trouble,
And be the first ones to head for the door!
Been there through it all?
The thick and the thin.
Some we may call family,
Others' we've labeled simply as friends!
Watching the pastor roll on by.
Gone be the deacons from the church!
Along comes a Good Samaritan
To wrap up the places that hurt!

Not looking at color or religion,
Just feeling the pain of me.
Not governed by denomination,
Or even deterred by what our differing political parties may be.
Simply did your best to help me!
Above and beyond!
Bringing such healing onto me
Only seeing in me by the power of God.
Hair or clothes not important to you
Thank you for not judging at all.
Seeing right through to the soul of truth
So many left, many others not even returned my call.
You walked, while your ride carried me!
Although I am an apparent contradiction to you!
You took time out, and decided to love me
Not even knowing what I would do.
For that I am forever grateful
Through you the love of God has shined through!
Your love has unhardened me.
And for that,
I am forever grateful to you.

"So he answered and said, you shall love the Lord your God with all your heart, with all your soul, with all your strength, and with all your mind, and your neighbor as yourself." Luke 10:27

GOD'S GOT IT

"But seek first the kingdom of God and His righteousness, and all these things shall be added to you"
Matthew 6:33

Cast away all of your cares!
Do not worry about.........A thing!
How much stature can we change with worry?
Focused on the renewing of the me;
Speaking only goodness through the mouth!
Searching about for riches and fame.
When in the end,
Gods got it!
Is what we find if we just call out and claim,
When we just call upon His name.
How to receive my blessing?
Bring it down swiftly from the sky.
Worried about the gas and rent
When by the heavens it is already provided!
How to open up the doors,
And close the ones not needed?
Leaving them swiftly behind.
Never again to have these proceedings:
Covered by the blood of Jesus!
Protected from all you try
Got to fight this fight to the ending;
Till the curtains close or we die,
Only God knows the final ending
Till then we remain positive.
Even when it all looks bad
Just know that God's got it.

MUCH OF WHAT I STUMBLED INTO BY FOLLOWING MY CURIOSITY AND INTUITION TURNED OUT TO BE PRICELESS LATER ON.

STEVE JOBS

WHAT YOU GOT LEFT

After the struggle,
At the end of all the heartache, grief, and pain.
Look around to see what's left,
What's not washed away in the pouring rain.
Purged away in the fire;
Burned free of all that we don't need.
Let's not bring this thing forward!
Won't try to reproduce the things that we don't need!
The cream will survive,
Dross sifted from the top.
Once all impurity has been burned away,
Look around to see what we've got.
Something must be left;
Not burned by the fire.
Take an inventory to see what is left
Some things that you never dreamed, pulled out of the mire.
This is what God will use!
Be fruitful and multiply this through me;
Compound what you got left,
Once all of the tears have streamed out of me.
The heat is no longer so hot
Crawled through the mud, and swam through the muck!
Barefooted out of the desert
Climbing over hot sand and rocks!
With no water and no pockets,
See you when you get to the top!
Now look around and see what you got;
Use this idle time to create what's already been in there
Dig deep
I bet you'll find your gift in there

STAND STILL

"Sun, stand still over Gibeon; and mourn, in the valley of Aijalow." 'So the sun stood still, and the moon stopped, till the people had revenge upon their enemies.'"

Joshua 10: 12-13

What type of thing have you fought?
Getting the best of you.
Scared of this thing.
Wondering how it is that you will will yourself through.
The decision to fight,
And force your way through.
Calling on control;
Willing to fight this battle, stronger than you ever knew!
Bring out the stone
And enclose my enemies soon.
You were the one chasing me,
And now here I am chasing you.
For the glory of God,
We'll bring restraint onto you
Just let me finish with this,
And then I'll be over there to deal with you.
Showing up over here,
When I know that's just where you bled through
Looking to find the source
Must first take care of the roots.
Just be still a little longer,
So all of mine enemies I can blow through.

FEEDING THE FEEDER

Why do I sit here thirsty?
Just taking up space!
The ox is what feeds me.
So why put a muzzle on its face!
Where do you spend your time?
Is it in what you reap?
If I give to you…
Why will you not give back unto me!
Paying this thing forward
This law of attraction onto me.
Where is it that I put my focus?
Look around to see what's come back to thee!
Been blessed with such blessings
Why to the swine do you take your seed?
Throwing this seed up into the air.
When it is this ground that feeds thee.
From whence shall you draw?
When it is time to eat?
Why take my pay
And spend with those who don't spend with me.
Giving back to the feeder
Even if it be not what was given onto me.
Call this here the barter system,
There is something that I have of importance 2 thee..
Can I give back what was drawn!
When this thing means so much to me,
But please take this....
I pray that it will do well for you,
Multiplied times more than what it has done for me.
Go to the tree to find feed,
Tell me what it is you see.
Why does this thing draw out nourishment?
If it will give back no seed.
My investment of time!
Put my energy into this tree.
Pruned and tilled,
Waiting for my time to eat.

This is my initial investment,
Must be careful what I chose to feed!
Who is there tearing me down!
And who is there looking to build the best of me?
Look to the left and to the right,
And see to who are we giving what.
How do we give so much hate and hurt
To those that give us so much love?

SOMETHING TO REACH FOR

This is the year
That I will decide to reach.
Knowing that there is manna
I must decide to just reach!
A reason to get out of bed!
A challenge that won't allow me to sleep!
Stretching my comfort zone,
Finding something that will bring out the best in me.
Overcoming the fear.
This thing I will conquest!
No time for lagging;
Must be the first one awake, and the last one to rest.
Finding this issue of fear
And deciding to be my best.
If it is that I must die anyway,
Might as well decide to kill it doing my best.
Facing these fears.
Putting the root of my problems to the test
Give me something to reach for,
Find me the reason to be my best.
In such a joyless place;
Putting depression to the test.
In such a barren land;
Still finding so much wet.
Poverty and violence
When well fed and peaceful Am I!
Infusing my spiritual warrior,
All with the power of my mind

WHEN IT HURTS BAD ENOUGH

When will I begin to praise?
How long before you begin to worship!
Not yet ready!
Would rather just keep on hurtin!
Why will we not give up the pain?
To the one who can take it all away!
If I just take him this little piece
He may decide to make my whole agony go away.

PLANTED NOT BURIED

What is the plan for you?
And why is it that you cannot see?
Planning and preparing,
But who is there to bring my increasing fold onto me!
Concealing this thing
In the hope of what it one day may be.
If I am but a small seed,
Before all is said and done, how many may I feed!
Covered by darkness
Wondering what this moisture could be!
Wondering if it's hurting,
Not sure that this flow is helping me!
Thank you for this protection;
This shallow cover about me.
Suspended in this place
Where the fowl won't use me for feed!
Waiting on my perfect moment
When I am no longer a seed in such need!
Deep down went my roots,
Until such an inward stretch came about from within me!
Grown from such a place
With so many odds stacked against me!
Knowing this is only possible
Because I spoke it against me!
Planted in such a place,
With the planter already knowing what I will be!
Tell me the difference!
Answer me why the world thought that it was burying me!
Not knowing my destiny,
Expecting you would bring an end to me!
I am much better now.,
It was necessary for me to be.
Building of my faith;
The physical man just can't see!
Because I sit in this dark place,
This still does not define me!
Waiting on my ultimate moment
Knowing it is my mind that truly defines the me.
Not the same as the I that went in,
This new beauty has come upon me!

Drawing upon these nutrients, until my time to bear seed!
Only will I praise,
Though all of these hardships continue to fall down on me!
In such a dry place,
What can be used to water thy dream?
Find me ready to cry;
"I am precious seed!"
Crying for so long,
Crying the self to sleep!
These collected tears
Are but water unto my hopeful dreams!
Dare not I quit!
Refusing to give in!
Knowing I will one day burst free.
If I just allow my will to be in alignment with His.

GROPING THROUGH THE DARK

"And now behold, the hand of the Lord is upon thee, and thou shalt be blind, not seeing the sun for a season, and immediately there fell on him a mist and a darkness; and he went about seeking some to lead him by the hand...."
Acts 136:16

See me in the darkness,
Looking to find my way.
Not sure of the direction we must go
Allowing the self to be led by faith.
How to not trip over this?
To not let that get in my way.
Reaching the hands to the front,
Hoping for a clear path to find my way!
Listening hard to see something;
Smelling my way back!
Senses in over drive; using all to find my way back.
Wondering will I ever get back?
Lights out with no mental picture!
My map to find solid growth, can anyone assess the bigger picture?
Has anyone sent out a search party?
Not lost, but I look to be unbound.
Traveling in unfamiliar territory
Not blinded, but just not yet found
A reason to slow down,
And take our sweet and precious time!
Who is there to blame?
Is your mother or father the reason that you were born maimed?
Can't put this deformity behind me,
Or try to place this infirmity on anyone else!
This done for God's Holy name;
For Her to show glory through Herself.
Who's watching this crisis?
Waiting for God's glory to shine through!
Not quite seeing the setup
This has been done for God to get His glory through.

"Now as Jesus passed by, He saw a man who was blind from birth. And his disciples asked him, saying, 'Rabbi, who sinned, this man or his parents, that he was born blind?'" John 9:1-2

ON THE DOWNSIDE

If my arrogance won't let me fall down
Then how to claim to believe in the resurrection!
If my chariot will only go north,
Then what point is it of the other directions?
Who would believe that when I went south
It was you allowing me to be pulled down?
Praising in your goodness,
But how many can rejoice when the chariots going down?
Hardened in the fire,
And cooled by the water:
The book of Job is a compass to me;
Abraham be more than a father.
Like David, we will be humbled,
And even Jesus went down!
Lazarus came forth!
But what if he was never bound?
This will be for the glory!
But first this thing must be done.
Some see this as the end,
I see one out planting the seed in the Son!
How to find the resurrection?
If not willing to be taken over by this storm.
In order to come up with all new garments,
Must learn to find joy while your suffering's on.
In what once was my darkest space,
Now lives faithfulness, goodness and self-control!
To imagine the ghetto that once inhabited this space.
To now that we know how to have community under control.
We already on the dowside.
Up is the direction we looking to go
We've already been on the downside
Upward will be our explosive growth.

SHORELINE

Where is it that you place your focus?
When you're out in the midst of the storm!
Fought so hard till you're almost in,
And then the fog comes along;
A sneaky deception.
Hindering your ability to physically see,
This is the time to keep on going,
Close your eyes, and allow the spiritual to be!
Focused on the destination,
Not on all the obstacles in between!
In my mind, already on the shoreline!
Although physically you cannot yet see me!

What makes your shoreline? And how far away could you be?
Been traveling these seas too long
To let the shallows now drown and overtake me.
How far is far enough;
When will this storm ever cease!
I keep on saying 'peace be still.'
Why is it that this does not seem to be working for me?
Attempting to settle the elements,
When truly we should be settling the self!
Jesus did it for God's glory.
Traveling out here alone,
Holding all belief in faith of self.

ALL BY FAITH!

Watch me grow through this,
In order to increase my faith!
Been given this blessing;
We have to use it or watch it waste away.
For the strength to just make it through this
Won't ask you to take it away.
How would you grow your muscles,
Without going to the gym every day?
In a test for endurance,
So I signed up for the race.
Not sure of what I would do,
So I started to train my faith!
Asked for patience, then all went crazy:
Wanted humility, then all was taken away!
Who has the manual?
The guide to help me see this thing through.
How to slim down?
And lose the excess weight too!
Trimming up the unbelief,
Pumping the self doubt away.
Running out this reprobate mind
Fasting the self-conceit away.
Needing to do it all away,
Until all that is left is faith.
Resistance bands and pushups!
Making self-ready for real weights.
Have to practice,
In order to grow this thing,
But in order to practice,
Must grow through those uncomfortable things.
Feeding the muscle ,
Multi Vitamins and supplemental things;
Watching these pastors on T.V.
And feeding the mind by the things we read!
Had to go through this,
Needed to test the faith!
Had to growth this first,
Before moving up to the higher place!

Who designed the foundation?
In the plans decided to first dig deep.
Be it stilts, bamboo, or concrete,
So much weight to go on top of that beam!
How much load can this base bear?
Looking to build this thing for strength;
How much is it that I can take.
For what reason did you design me like this?
Why must I go through this?
Why can't this thing be easier?
Can't you just up and take me away?
How much is this thing designed to bear?
Gravity alone already places so much weight!
This atmosphere displaces so much wait.
Hurry up and get me to the destination,
So I can just put this thing away.
Yoked by this thing for so long!
Is that you on the other side of this drone?
Or am I out here walking and talking all alone!
Cultivating the Master's land,
In this time of deep discovery
Willing to find out how much power is spoke in man,
If only the strong are allowed to be.
Who designed me to be this way?
I die daily!
Just have to wake up to die just one more day in here.
To find your grace to be sufficient
More enduring than my every need by faith.
Safe in the midst of this storm
Awaiting my eruption date!

THE ONLY LIMIT TO OUR REALIZATION OF TOMORROW
WILL BE OUR DOUBTS OF TODAY. LET US MOVE FORWARD
WITH STRONG AND ACTIVE FAITH.

FRANKLIN ROOSEVELT

WHEN FEAR IS THE LOUDEST

How is it that you will get through?
When so much has you scared.
Not sure how to go on.
Not certain that anyone will be there.
Who will you turn to
When you find the self hypnotized by fear.
Caught in this trance!
Can't speak, can't run, and can't hear!
How many have received bad news?
The cancer looks to be so near.
Where will money come from to pay the rent?
When will I ever get out of here?
Who will get the job?
What if I put it all into this stock?
Who can tell me if it will go up?
And who can tell me when it will drop!
Have you ever been afraid in your mind;
Too afraid to open the door!
Tell me how to move such a mountain?
With all of this ice and snow!
How long before we find the corect way?
headed to sure!
As for me and my house
We will serve the Lord.
When all around looks so crazy
When we're right in the middle of the storm!
The night looks so dark
Right before the dawn comes along.
Just when I was ready to give up,
Along came the reason to carry on.
Spinning around my everything!
Who knew a whirlwind would be the reason?
Turned all of this upside down;
Growing by what it fed upon
In the spiritual, who will be there to lead us?
Keep us moving forward when the fear is the loudest.
Quieting the unbelief
Only visual atop that mountain

THE SON WILL ALWAYS

Who is there to lead by example?
From where comes the heat to keep thee warm!
Been going through the midst of such revolution,
Who will keep me safe in the storm.

THANK YOU FOR THE STORM

Going through this turmoil;
So many believe it death to me!
Got the heart of a warrior,
And an uncanny ability to want to succeed!
I encourage you to have no empathy,
No sympathy for me.
I was born to be a soldier;
This situation will turn out to be a positive one, you'll see.
Not afraid of the challenge
Or deterred by what's been born!
In me is an innate ability
A crazy belief that wakes me for another morn.
When so many would have given up!
Found the reasons to keep moving on.
What exactly is there, that will keep you moving strong?
Something bigger than the self,
A greater cause than me!
Something in which I can throw myself,
Give to something more than just me.
With all of the thunder and lightning
How to think of something that is far beyond me?
In the depths of my fear
How am I to comfort thee?
In the wind and the rain thine own spoken will be done.
Will this thing ever end?
Now the ground is beginning to become like muck;
Feet beginning to sink in.
Stepping through the cold,
Prepared for the fight!
Look into my face,
On my beard and eyelashes see all of this ice and snow?
Such a refusal to quit.
Never willing to give in!
It was in me the whole time
The ability to do this shit!
But it took such a storm
To lock me in.

WHEN THE HEDGE IS OFF

"And the Lord said unto satan, behold, all that he hath is in thy power, only upon himself put not forth thine hand……." Job 1:12

What is there to do, when She takes off this angelic ring?
Praying for protection!
When She has already allowed me to run free!
Free to take everything; have all except for me.
Cannot touch my soul. Cannot take away my being!
Will I be the one to give up? When all's not going the way that I think.
Thinking back to Jesus in the wilderness.
How many have been through such a thing?
Not only just me.
So many have already passed through this way.
Allowed to put me through the test;
Checking on the diligence of my faith.
Who can make it when the fence is off? Halo let down!
No fire wall around thee.
Take off the cheat code now.
Force field taken down,
Maginot line no more!
Nothing to take down, just some of this boasting.
Attacks upon the mind; Body and soul!
How much faith do you have to proceed in the way?
How much strength do you need, to keep moving on toward the goal?
God said 'this is the way'
Although it does not seem to be.
Moving so close to my release date
And still I feel so far from being free!
What is there that protects this life?
Madness all about me
Count how many I've seen lose life.
Passing through this place that I must be.
Exposed to the lions,
Like Daniel I am God's favorite Sun.
Just a drop from a bucket!
A ray of light touching the skin,
Sent shining down by the Son.
Who is the daughter of greatness?
Led by the great spirit of I AM.
Walking on into the end of this
What we speak through life
Is what we manifest in the end.

WE'RE ON THE MOVE

How is it that you can stop us?
Try to hold His people down.
Still smiling and dancing,
Those who endure shall wear the crown.
Tried your best to defeat me,
Beat me while I was down!
The plan is for an intended end.
Can't get caught up in what we see right now.
Still we walk by faith,
Not deceived by sight!
Just got to keep on moving.
There ain't no stopping us tonight.
However did we get here
And how to move where She wants us to be?
The master of illusion!
The murderer, wrecking ball, and thief;
Won't damper my vision, or destroy my belief.
Given this vision, and told to, 'Only believe!'
Never would the world think
That after this you'd still use me.
No loss of zeal! We won't settle unto defeat.
The path is narrow! And
Although it's ugly, this is exactly where She needs us to be.
Humbled by misdirection,
Jonah is the same as me.
Had to find myself,
While sitting in the belly of the beast.
Decided not to ever give up
Even on those long, cold nights with no heat.
They went through the wilderness
As did Jesus while He didn't even eat.
How many of us spoiled in the wilderness?
Given so much food to eat.
Yet we take all for granted
Instead of being grateful for what we receive!
No, I'd rather just sleep.......

Wake up everybody no more sleeping in bed!
I believe we can make a difference,
Form a voice for those unjustly dead.
We are on the move now,
And by faith, there ain't no stopping us.
Never can we settle to defeat
The King is rerouting us!
Preset the G.P.S.
My navigation has been found.
Must muster up the strength,
It's gonna take courage and strength,
Time to do things different now!
No more of who we were back then,
Masters of the impossible!
The way the world turns
Is all determined by my thoughts right now.

How much power do we have?
And divide that by how much of that we use?
Will win by will power
And all of the glory is given to You!!

MAKE IT STOP

Got me afraid to leave prison!
In here I find it safe!
Turn on the T.V. one dead;
Resemblance to my face!
Who is there that will end this?
Long ago war was already declared:
War on drugs;
War on crime!
Can we put war on this hunger we hear rumbling?
An end to those having no beds?
Bring resources to where cupboards are currently bare!
Talk to my people on top!
Outrage to the ones in control!
My people out here can't even protest
Without the fear of, by our own military, being turned cold.
Steadily training the authority,
Military weapons used on our shores!
Imagining those killed looking like you;
Regicide at your back door!
How quick would this thing be through!
Put an end to it all by force!
jim crow continues to speak!
Sitting back laughing, How long has it been
Since his last words were wrote?
No more lynching. So you now blast me;
Choked out cold, out on the street! What are we right now doing?
Based upon what history has done to me!
How do we close this door? Fight fire with fire!
Just one morning of hours left to purge!
Not all are evil! But so many are corrupt
That are in control; Those in control,
Any resemblance to me!
Jury of my peers?
Who in there that looks anything like me?
The jury says not guilty!
Without the badge, it's murder in cold blood!
Death to your civil suit!
Terrorist, right here on our own shore!
What is it that they're fighting for?
Why do so many want to blow down the doors!
My history will never repeat
No more gunned down on the floor.

INTUITION IS GIVEN ONLY TO HIM

WHO HAS UNDERGONE LONG

PREPARATION TO RECEIVE IT.

LOUIS PASTEUR

SHE'S ENOUGH

When the want is to do something different,
Represented by less than my best
It is her love that gives me the reason,
The strength to bring out my best.
Life moves in many directions;
With her love I'm comfortable at rest.
Not anxious nor nervous,
Patient and at rest!
In all individuals, only seeing the best.
Once was addicted,
Now love is the most powerful drug.
Used to be conflicted,
Now these decisions are grounded in love.
Not afraid of this good feeling,
Nor embarrassed by peers that laugh,
Glad to be caking
Thankful for this love that lasts.
How much good will come about?
When we always put our love first?
More important than anything
Honesty always to cum first.
Decided to love more
When life's circumstances bring us down!
Bounded by everything
This binding won't be broken down!
Why try so hard to kill it!
If this not be a good thing!
So many want to end it
By God I only focused on this intended end.
Cumming through victorious:
Our love in the end.
With each day to keep trying,
And our love will win.

MY DEMISE

Happily ever after
Till death do us part!
The only one I've ever felt totally free with.
How does it feel to have all of my heart?
Walk over my body,
Trample my soul!
Sorry I can't be there to put my arms around you
When the nights become cold.
You've always been the one to comfort me,
No one else can put my mind at ease.
How now do you not give a damn!
Worked so hard on this love too not leave.
Tell me what happened to us?
How did we fall so far apart?
Controlling and demanding!
I've given you all of my heart!
Wanting to know about your everything
Because you are mine.
Death to what used to be,
Seen rolling by in that long car.
From excited to have my child,
To birth control should be!
Guess we'll just bring back the condoms,
Why even did you marry me?
Given you me! My heart, my soul, my all of me.
How did it ever come to this?
You won't even answer my calls.
Make me know there's no one else
What more could there be!
Giving him all the good loving
All of the attention that you used to give to me.
How did we even come to this?
Never seen the fall!
All couples go through this?
The Holy Spirit speaks.
Convicting the consciousness
Can we just be honest while we speak?
If this love is no longer what you want
Then we would have no choice but to leave!

VALUE

Why would there be a robbery
If inside there is no wealth?
What is there to take from you?
If you have nothing left!
Growing along with the tare;
Stealing from the wheat.
Tell me who is this attack upon?
And why does so much of it get released upon me?
So valuable to my owner,
So you decide to attack.
Just grown upon this soul,
So you try to use me to get Him back!
Planted with intention
So you notice my growth.
Counted of His inheritance
So you want to stop it while it's still unknown.
What weed killer can take you away?
How much miracle growth can unhinder me?
It wasn't until God planted
That you came to attack me.
Keep on trying to rob me.
Though it hurts so much!
Attacking from every direction, but still I won't give up!
40 days in the wilderness; such an unusual attack.
Still here with a smile on my face
Just waiting to get back!
Give Him a praise,
Like one never before seen!
Been through the depths of hell
And still chose to serve my King.

(Untitled)

"But when the grain had sprouted and produced a crop, then the tares also appeared."

Matthew 13:26

Praying for such blessings!
Not sure what they may come with.
Wanting the honey and flowers,
But not sure what the hibiscus may come with!
Asking God to take thee to the sky;
Landed down in the pit!
With all of my hopes and dreams
How did I end up in this?
Not what I prayed to get!
Or where I envisioned the promised land to be,
Over there stuck out in the wilderness;
Even Jesus had to go through this; The likeness onto he!
Much pain, just had to live through.
How do we meet such pleasure?
Ask me why is it that I praise so much.
By what I've been through, I've earned this letter.

GIVE ME SOMETHING

What is this thing that you need, in order to fight back?
By God given to thee
As a means to defend against attack:
Pot of oil;
The jawbone of an ass;
5 loaves and 2 fish.
My God delights in giving us unusual gifts.
Just don't let the things you're sent, decay in mass.
When it is your time, She will release the blessing;
Thing needed to help you get across that next pass.
What is it that we will do?
Tithing to cast down the high things that can cause us stress.
Bringing my offering unto you
Your reward is safe in thine cache chest;
I will give all back to you.
Selling all that I have!
Giving my last two mites unto you!
Unto these things no connection do I have.
All of the glory! I give unto you.
What is it that you worship!
Holding it higher than God to you.
In the midst of your climb
Keeping that thing in mind,
Watch out so of it, you don't become robbed of your mind;
A loosing of the self in time,
Who will still do? Even when the things are taken away!
When the things all begin to come in, what is it
That you will give away!
Given the gold,
But with it what will you make?
Worshipping such idols
Things made by man, not formed of God's way.
Trust God and believe in God's plan;
Blessed to shine through the power of good!
The almighty is upon me
All else will attract to the friend of good!

I Am HE;
Hallelujah, and praise to Allah!
Bowing my profit to His purpose
All of this cattle by the power of the mind!
Making the resource to worship.
Bow down to the power of Him
Stepping into such a blessing,
But my soul it won't take in this mist.
Blessed to be a blessing
Sharing His all with you!
Got the grace to be grounded
Humbled in what God is getting ready to do.

"..........Hast not thou made an hedge about him, and about his house, and about all that he hath on every side? Thou hast blessed the work of his hands, and his substance is increased in the land...."

Job 1:10

LOOK IN THAT CUP

"Then came to him the mother of Zebedee's children with her sons, worshipping him, and desiring a certain thing of him." St. Matthew 20:20

Have you ever asked for something?
And found out you really didn't even need it?
Begging and pleading
Thinking you're mature enough for this thing
That you think you're believing in!
How many times have you gotten it?
And found out that it was just too much?
Not quite what you hoped for
It was just not even enough!
Have you ever claimed the promise?
Before you took the time out to research the process.
Focused on the seat,
Blind to how many steps it took to mount the chair!
What is it that you're right now asking for?
Now look at what you're right now going through.
The path to the position!
The route that we must go through.
Not knowing what we ask for
First look in the cup!
Blinded by the allure,
But can't see the process in which it takes to fill it up!
First go and do the research,
And see what they had to give up:
Mocked; scourged; and crucified.
What are you willing to give up?
If to him whom much is given
So much the more required!
Washing the outside of the cup,
When it's the inside that is filled with all the muck and mire

UNWANTED

Who is there that wants me?
For what purpose do I fit a need?
Down here at my lowest.
And not even those I love seem to love me.
What am I to do?
Not going down how I seen this to be.
The power of a hug?
A phone call to say that you love me.
How does a wife no longer know you?
Kids not want you to be!
"Keeping families together!";
Promise made by the M.D.O.C
Discarded with the garbage
Digging to find the strength in me
Love me when I'm back,
Right now you just can't see.
How do I show you my love?
Teach you to care;
Even to those who may of wronged you, to show some empathy
To have some compassion and care.
No, not to be stupid,
But when a woman is down
Who is there to hold her hand,
Helping her to get up from there.
Moving on to the next stand,
I see you as my neighbor in love.
You throw me out with the trash.
Already see the ending to this,
You're gonna want me back
Maybe even find me needed for this.

DARKNESS

"Woe unto you that desire the day of the Lord! To what end is it for you? The day of the Lord is darkness and not light. As if a man did flee from a lion, and a bear met him; or went into the house, and leaned his hand on the wall, and a serpent bit him. Shall not the day of the lord be darkness, and not light? Even very dark, and no brightness in it."

Amos 5:18-20

How many of us are running for goodness?
Instead of embracing the pain!
Rather than hoping for a sunny day,
Go on out and dance in the rain.
Thinking because my world is dark,
That God doesn't love me.
Or because this thing is bad, that God doesn't long for me.
His thoughts are higher than our thoughts,
His ways higher than our ways.
I think we're going the wrong way
If we're all thinking the same thang!
I see God in the prison cell;
Jesus wearing the same chains!
I hear His voice in the confusion out on the prison yard!
John lived through the same thing!
Feel God in this affliction
Though it's not in years of blood!
Know God when the rent is due.
The blind man waited outside in love.
Who will have compassion on the innocent?
Jacob was given a continuance as well!
Empathy for the captors:
Paul converted those filled with hate onto the living well!
Show me an instance of darkness,
And I'll show you why for God it was an instance for light!
Ruth went to glean behind the reapers!
Well I can begin to use the food stamps on my card tonight!!
You stand there and judge!
Just look at what we got out of this life.
A diaspora of seed,
In the darkness planting seeds of light.
Darkness and rain: Fertile grounds for the gain.

81

Jonah fleeing to Tarshish,
Have you ever went the wrong way?
Base life in similarities, comparisons to those of the past!
Thanks 2 Pac, Dr. Martin Luther King Jr., and Malcolm X,
Darkness had to come in order for you to get passed.
Treyvon left for greatness.
So many other seeds cum unnamed.
Planting a harvest of greatness,
Just as soon as the soil is set again.
Tilled to be its best,
All you see is darkness.
But your light shall illuminate the way for the rest.
Because of you, we have light to make it through this gauntlet.
Who coulda guessed the dark tunnel was the way?
All others went to the light,
We began the dark and narrow way
Never given the chance to choose the light

UNDER THE HEAVY HAND OF OPPRESSION

"Jesus answered and said unto him, because I said unto thee, I saw thee under the fig tree, believest thou? Thou shalt see greater things than these. And He saith unto him, verily verily, I say unto you, hereafter ye shall see heaven open, and the Angels of God ascending and descending upon the son of man."
St John 15; 50-51

Under whose fig tree do you now sit?
What holds you down?
Am I here to find shade,
Or when you look down deep are you secretly bound!
Could this be this same one? The one that produced no figs!
Does this really hold me down?
Though I believe I'm gaining benefit from it:
Who is there to rationalize, a human taken down?
Shot by the protectors
And the world moves on like no ones missing!
An end to the lynching, Thank you Lord!
Who would rationalize if a Black police, shot onea yours!
Separate but equal.
Equally separate.
All lives matter!
Is anyone looking at it from a different perception!
Is anyone looking from the outside into this disaster?
To truly see objectively through the chatter!
Will the day ever come?
When you see me as I see you!
Aint I a brother! I am much more than chattle!
Simply an animal to you.
No longer is this 1922!
Why the same ignorance?
Back around full cycle,
If I get get mad I'm an animal,
But its o.k. for you to just kill us when you're hurting.
Give me the statistics of the Black male who aint home!
Please just take accountability from here.
You broke up these homes.
You separated these kids.
Now call it ironic, and label me as a deadbeat!
This is a path you set
Way back in 1833.

An end to civil war
Thanks to all who fought for me.
Know now that I stand up in pride
Thankful for who I've come to be.
Separation to be the matter, since the 16th century
Centuries date back of you, taking my Father away from me.
I believe in ghosts
Memories floating from the distant past!
A trend has been created!
In my mind I can hear jim crow clap!

An end to the years!
Those 400 years coming up to being done!
It's time for us to create change

A new generation must be begun!
Won not bound by the past.
Time to create our own group think,
Build a legacy that will last; one that is all our own thing!
Searching through your prisons!
Break free all of my political leaders!
It's been quiet for so long!
We have none brave enough to lead us!

To erase the ignorance, we must band together for peace
No longer willing to fight
Just want to live in peace!!
It's still a fight!
Check the conundrum in fighting for a good cause!
Living my life for peace!
Though currently I reside under the wait of the lost.

4 EVERY STEP

Thank you Lord for this movement
From here to over there!
Pain in my back,
Aches in my knees,
Yet and still, I don't even care.
Just thankful for this movement
No need of a chair!
Don't want you to wheel me!
My God will allow me to get out of there.
All for His glory
No credit given to these swollen ankles and feet!
Just gotta keep praising God
For each inch closer that we can reach.
Ready to dance!
Won't let the pain stop me!
Through it all God has a special place for us,
To lie with the king: Ready to get there?
And won't stop until it comes to be.
Even when we have to stop and look back,
Acknowledging how much ground has been covered behind me.
Remembering when I was back there
Wondering how ever could I get this all behind me?
'Just one more step'
I continually hear you whisper from beyond!
Finding the strength!
Can't wait until the pain dies from the inside.
In the midst of the storm,
Still you wouldn't let the heavy rains stop me.
Urged me to keep on stepping! Thank you Lord that you didn't
leave me. Had to keep on moving,
Climbing to where only in my mind's eye could see.
Beyond the pain and the murk!
Just kept me moving through the deep.
Rain drops falling down, tasting so good to me.
Out in the wind, and out in the cold!
Through the slush and the snow.
Just gotta keep on going,
Thank you Lord for all of this growth!
Thanks for the new plants that we have here.
With each and every step.
I smell home becoming nearer and nearer with every single breath.

FOR CHANGE

"And he answered and spake unto those that stood before Him, saying, take away thine iniquity to pass from thee, and I will clothe thee with change of raiment."
Zechariah 3:4

Bring me the different!
An end to the old me.
Change my nature, change my garments,
Place your new mind upon me.
No longer who I was, no longer what I used to be.
From the inside, through the outside
How much strain does this new thing bring onto me?
Moody and uncontrollable
Discomforted in growth.
The ultimate plan you have for me
I currently just dont know.
A branch off of what I used to be
Grafted unto this new thing.
Nothing that could happen overnight.
This thing had to first bring about such pain and grief.
Filthy on the inside,
Dirty and dingy on the out.
After leaving such a dirty place
How in such glee does one come about?
Glowing and illuminated,
A reflection of such precious light.
Jesus, change my name!
Please get my garments right!

BUILT FOR THIS TIME

Look at all that I've been through
What the past has brought to pass!
Born in a broken home,
Single parent mother playing dad!
Through gangs and street violence;
Beyond drugs and alcohol how did I last!
Against all odds into college.
Graduated near the bottom of the class!
A walk on to the football team,
How many could have completed this dream?
Never would have known this was just me learning,
How to become me.
So young and teaching college students,
Who could have ever seen this in me!
Went on to become a member,
Of the Indiana State Police.
So much resolve in doing that,
Moral, respectful, and a man of integrity;
Now how in prison here I sit.
However could this come to be?
This whole path has just been strength for me.
Never would have made it.....
Been put away for this long
In here I sit to find strength to take it.
How else to grow this strong!
Built for this perfect moment I got.
Created for this perfect position in time!
Necessary for me to take up my lot.
Built for this perfect time.
In this perfect place

AFTER EFFECTS

Have you ever been hit?
Punched right in the eye!
Kicked in the leg!
Broken a bone?
Found yourself with dry eyes, ready to cry!
Remembering being stung by a bee,
Or thinking back to how you found out you were allergic to
That thing!
The initial punch is shocking!
The first poke will hurt.
Paralyzed by a foot to the leg,
Traumatized by a slide in the dirt.
How necessary is the ice?
When you find out you twisted an ankle.
Asleep for the surgery,
But how to soar again after the waking?
Found in this situation
That we're dealing with seven years later!
Ten to twenty more years
And still some things may be in danger.
Wanting this fixed right away!
But needing to give this healing some more time!
The after may hurt even more than the initial.
But by faith,
Healing will come in time.
How many would believe that this day would ever come?
It was seven short years ago.
They wanted to convince me that your time was done,
Standing on top of my nose!
Refusing to be afraid!
Nothing more I could do, but use this all for faith!
Go ahead,
Unplug the machines;
The just shall live by faith!
The real outcome is the aftereffects
When all of the initial fades away.
Don't worry all, She only sleeps.
Once you unplug She will awake!
All for God's glory.
Where is it that you've placed your faith.
Can't even be there physically
But spiritually you are lighting the way.

DEAD

What is this bright light?
Flashing before my eyes.
Glimpses and images keep showing
So much happens in prison; and life rides right on bye.
Hot water and grease, will leave one hell of a scar!
Grandma's funeral; Why did I freeze in that crowd?
Me as a professor,
Indiana State Police!
Changing diapers and cooking dinner,
Is this the life for me?
Snow forts and dog walks,
Running through the house.
Michigan Football!
From high school, who ever would of thought?
Smoking weed and selling dope!
Running in and out of momma's door;
Running these streets!
The good or the bad?
What does this life have in store?
Label me as a mess-up,
Here I am with my second wife!
What must it take
For me to be the best man that I've ever been in my life?
Thinking back on these images,
Death to he!
Looking on to the future,
Time for me to be birthed on through She.
Locked away for so long
Can't wait to once again just be me!
For this time to just move along.
How long before a hug be free?
To show that love is still what governs me.
Still the great man that I was.
Gonna need you to take time and re get to know me.
Been gone for so long. I know you no longer know me,
That old man is gone

THROUGH THE STORM

Have you ever found yourself trekking through the darkness?
Outside in the dark all alone.
So much cold and wind involved with this.
How to see the sun and the moon as reference points to get home!
Walking with head down,
Only to shield the eyes from the blowing snow.
Praying for goodness,
Wishing goodness go up in a puff of smoke.
Against the grain,
Watch as I continue to climb
Thought about resting here;
Just gotta keep on moving,
In order to get back to mine.
Won't give in
No matter how much we get knocked down.
Out here with no thermos or under clothes.
Still won't wear a frown.
Expecting to receive goodness
Refusal to be down!
Thought I would just give up,
Because you continually beat me down!
Just not enough;
Refusal to ever quit
As long as the heart is pumping and thumping
Brings heat to the inside of this.
In the midst of confusion,
How many will still keep the faith?
Find me in here sleeping
While so many complain the time away!
Panic is not a strategy;
I go to my solitude room to pray!
Just because it didn't happen right now.
Doesn't mean that it won't happen later on today.
Whose perception of time
Will wash this fear away!
My God is eternal
So why ever would I fear today?

JUDGMENT

How do I define myself?
Why do I compare you onto me?
Looking to see highly of myself,
So that I can find the height in me.
By finding the fault in you!
What makes my situation so Holy?
My circumstances more important than yours!
Imagine how Joseph felt:
God told him, Don't worry, she carries the Lord!
Doing everything right,
And out of wedlock for this child to be born.
Everyone to see you as a sinner;
When she's never even known you!
Moses taking mans life,
And from that look who he came into!
David. A man after God's own heart,
And just how imperfect was he?
How great is our God!
Who will get to be the next to use such human error for the whole's belief?
No I'll never do this again,
But thank you God, that this happened as it should!
From a man of the law
To locked up is me!
Find me on Google or Twitter, take the time out to read the feeds!
This is all for God's own glory!
No time for woe is me.
Must keep the head held high
And become what God has destined in the end for me to be!
Not tangled up in a fault,
Or bogged down by mistakes
No this is not the end of the line.
We're just getting there another way!

IN THE BREAKING!

"And when he had taken the five loaves and the two fish, he looked up to Heaven, Blessed and broke the loaves, and gave them to his disciples to set before them; and the two fish he divided among them all."
Mark 6:41

Thank you for the cursing,
For kicking me to the side!
Giving up such heartache,
When we thought it was time for life!
Needing to be broken! For the multiplication to happen!
Though Jesus broke it!
It was the disciples who did the passing!
Where must it come from?
At the end of whose hands!
Thank you for breaking me Lord.
Knowing this is all part of your bigger plan!
Even when it feels as if it's just not enough,
I will still thank you Lord!

Appreciative for the blessing,
Thankful for what has come by your love!
Thank you for breaking me Lord
Making me this changed man.

Living forever free
No matter how often they put these cuffs on my hands!
Who called this a breaking?
Label this as my coming out party;
Trying to kill my inner man.
Find me so much stronger and hearty;
Finding God's strength, in such a troublesome land!
Thankful for the breaking!
Not afraid for what was taken out of my hand.
Grateful that you brought me through this, just one more
Reference point along the plan: Bear paws and lions teeth;
They chained me y'all.
Left me down in this pit,
Expected the lion to dismantle the god.
Unable to see the way!
Just know I ain't dead!
Couldn't make it no longer!
And all that came,
Was a little bit longer!

92

THE WAY TO SEE FAITH IS TO SHUT THE EYE

OF REASON.

BEN FRANKLIN

Blessings clothed in hardships
Favor adorned in misery!
Who can find the glisten?
Even when hard times attempt to overtake thee?
In the midst of such a storm
Not sure of what the outcome will be.
Still you see strength,
When you look over here at me!
Living above this confusion
Trying not to let fear get the best of me!
Living by faith;
Refusing to back down because of what I see!
An intended destination!
That may not work.
Why decide to keep going;
So many dreams seen riding by in a hearse!
Why should such greatness be born?
In such a dirty space!
Told to have favor,
And still hiding in such a wicked place!
How many will come for the celebration?
That couldn't endure the whole fight!
So easy when the kids are so perfect,
But what about when they are hard headed and don't listen right?
Purposely doing nothing right.
Parents out here lost. Confused in this dance with place and time.
Unable to plug into our kids, feeling as if we can do nothing right,
But God has a plan.
Who says His strategy would be easy?
Trusted with the light of the world,
And everything has gone into a whole new way of believing!
Picked to fulfill this destiny!
Traveling this Road that I dare not know.
When they told me this is the way to favor!
No warning of the difficulties lying down this road!
Does my fear negate my faith?
My hardships deny my life's destiny?
Because it does not work out perfect,
Does it mean that She's not here blessing me?
Because we go through such a dark storm

Practicing the will to never quit!
Who will dare continue to love!
When placed in the midst of all of this!
Feeling to be in the pit of hell,
To be forced to live in a place such as this.
Yet I will still show face.
Through whatever difficulties,
Will never give up on this love
That She gives.

YOU WERE STILL THERE

"Be strong and of good courage, do not fear nor be afraid of them; for the lord your God, He is the one who goes with you. He will not leave you nor forsake you."

Deuteronomy 31:6

When all else had gone;
To be seen, there was none left.
Here is my time on trial,
Facing what you may call my untimely death.
An end of me;
Death to the me that you know!
Standing here lost and confused,
Shackled, in these cuffs on the floor.
Wondering for family
Who is there to call my best friend?
Few and far in between,
Approximately ten helping hands!
Borrow in the physical realm,
But in the spiritual the bank is full.
There is One here standing next to me,
And He knows exactly what to do.
You may see me as a loser
For this here that we must go through!
The angels in here celebrating!
Already knowing what the Lord is about to do!
Can't see the big picture,
Too focused on the limited view.
How many are in the furnace?
Who else is there in that pit with these lions too!
Who else is there in that pit, standing strong for you?
When all else had given up
You are the One who stayed true.
Watching me scream out, but never giving up in my confusion!
Wandering why it is that you're not here!
How many know how to look to the spiritual?
In order, through the physical, you will get through with this.
When all else failed,
It is You who stood through this.
In my soul there is nothing left,
And yet you are still here.

STAY

This right here is my destiny.
You were made to be my Wife.
No matter what this world may bring,
You are my soul mate!
Gods perfect creation;
The other whole unto me, my wife.
Adjoined to you through eternity,
For how many years, for you, have I been willing to wait?
Decades of knowing you were meant to be in my life.
Finally to meet my favor;
Through such wrong,
How could come about something so right?
Thank you for all of you,
Grateful to be the one to give you my kiss.
Thank you for practicing such patience
Waiting for our soul to once again evade time.
Free!
Perfect in conversation,
Made for me in this life,
You are my rib, my partner, my life.
By God! Love like yours could not be bought.
Giving you all of me.
So open to spots that I never before knew.
Never will you again be away from me;
My soul glued unto you!
"Never let someone else determine the direction your life takes,
Never let someone else create you."
Thank you for deciding to stay

WHEN LOVE IS FOUND

"I don't want to fall in love, I want to grow in love every single day."

How many mundane things
Do we pass through each and every day?
Taking a shower, brushing your teeth,
Sitting down to relax at the end of the day.
Who will find joy
In washing clothes or shoveling snow?
Do you look forward,
To simply going to the grocery store?
The power in date night,
Joy from opening the car door!
Only to stare in eyes,
Simply to hold you; body close to mine.
Cleaning the gutters, and cutting the grass, me and you!
A walk in the park, holding hands out in the dark.
Thank you God for Public displays of affection;
Show me how much you seared me in your heart.
Thank you for everything,
Or for nothing at all!
Only to have your breath on me,
Means everything because you are my all.

WHEN MY SOUL SCREAMS

When my body has to be quiet,
Yet my spirit is screaming to be free!
Close my eyes and hear my soul cry;
Inside screaming out to the King!
Troublesome to be these waters;
Here the blessing may be.
Deciding to change my own perspective,
Sending these praises up to the King.
Been here in need of this storm,
How many will agree?
Wanting to live this burden,
Knowing that it all starts within me.
The journey of 3,000 days,
All to begin with one single day's death.
Using these gifts that God has given
To answer the call of the best!
No longer afraid to stand up,
Or sit down when humbleness must be!
Body still,
Mind quiet,
And soul at ease.
And here it is when my soul begins to scream.
Looking to find the true me.

HEAVY IS THE HEAD

Who dares to put on this helmet?
To hold up the weight that it bears down!
How heavy are these gold and diamonds?
Rubies and gems laced all around!
How many ounces of gold
Is to be sufficient to be labeled a crown?
Strong shoulders!
Strong back.
How much pressure can these legs press up from the ground:

Cancer scares,
And pulled paroles.
How many more must die?
So many deaths come and gone
From a baby to a child!
What do you deem necessary?
Needed to fuel this growth.
This place where you need me to be
What if I'm not strong enough yet to go?
Not enough resolve to get where you want me to be!
How many will dare to stand here?
Lonely at the top! Have to practice resiliency,
A long way from where I used to be;
Straight from the bottom to the top!
The wait of this robe.
The breath of these furs!
Who is willing to go through,
What it takes to live inside of here?
To move about up and down these stairs!
To sit upon His throne!
How to know what one has gone through
In order to get to sit on that throne?
You only see when all is done and through,
Paying attention to the glamor and glory,
But how many places of exile have you been to?
Sitting alone in the darkness,
Still singing praise songs up to you in glory
Finding the faith not to run!
How many have been tried?

If you dare come in to take the crown;
Come with your army plus mine.
Refusing to give in, never backing down.
Even after I tried hard, and still fell down.
Bruised knees and bloody elbows!
Never will I let my kingdom down!
So many wish to be like me,
But how many can bear the wait of this crown?

BLOCKING MY RELEASE

So much that I have to give;
How much is there to receive?
Everyone has a want to have;
How many are there to give onto others' needs?
Taking this and taking this;
Pressed beyond measure and belief.
Mentally tired and physically exhausted.
How to maintain when both of them are upon me?
Under pressure!
When so much does not have to be.
So many things coming in
Why must you block my release?
Creating a situation, where you will expect me to blow!
If anyone lived under this, so many would have already gone.
Taking the time out to think,
After we've already gone!
What if I could just take the time?
And walk away from all of my needs.
Looking for an outlet.
A way to let it all go.
Up way passed My boiling point,
And this thermometer continues to grow.
Knowing that I am well over hot,
Why must you still make me heat!
It's so easy to blow
Must have a hole for the crockpot to release.
Fit for the Fight
What do you do?
When all that you plan don't go right?
Committed to a thing
Believing in it with the all of you.
What to do with disappointment?
Heartache? Weariness in well doing?
Moving forward in strength,
Or letting bitterness in this rule you!
Moving in passed my breaking point
No longer exhausted by what I've been through.
The more obstacles you send
The more I find out how hard I can try.

Battle tested and built to endure,
Battered and bruised!
Mind still going,
So the body refuses to lose.
Threw me away,
But I didn't throw in the towel.
Didn't hear no bell ring,
Just kept fighting hard;
Even when I didn't know how!
Where is the finish line?
I swear to God it just moved.
No, I still won't cry!
More time to spread the good news.

WHAT IF GOD LIVES IN YOUR SHADOW

Thank you David Banner
For exposing me to the light.
How many will spend our whole life searching,
Looking outside for inner light?
Running from our own darknesses
Afraid of what might be there.
Being followed by this the whole time alone,
And not even aware that it's there.
Who is there to expose me to this?
Teach me of this being!
Finding light in the darkness
What an amazing thing!
So simple in theory;
It is in darkness that light shines all the more.
How many times when we cannot see?
Do we run quickly back out of the door!
Afraid to be in this thing
Because physically we can't see.
When I close my eyes and look through the spirit,
This is exactly where I needed to be.
Afraid to bring Him my darkness;
How will He bring about my light unto me?
The Profit is sent for the sick!
Those who need to believe in His being.
What is this thing?
Following me around the whole time.
Always right here behind,
No matter where it is that I climb.
No matter how low I may go,
In the depths of despair, and darkness;
Still there.
At my highs and at my lows
Always right here.
Exactly where I'm embarrassed to be.
Looking out into the sun
The whole time you're right there with me.
No where to run

HAPPYNESS DEPENDS ON OURSELVES
ARISTOTLE

WHY FREE THE SLAVE?

White, Black, Mexican, and Native American they come in all colors,
But let's face reality. This is a place we will always be the minority.
From Africa to the New world, France, Europe and Asia.
This exportation is big business!
The whole world wants to take us.
Free labor! And the only cost is human nature:
These aren't people anyway: snatch out
Their teeth; and put marks on them
So we can claim them.
Leave them out in the field from dust to dust;
My production is up 110,185% from last spring to this one!
Bring me all you got; I'll put them all to work
The cost for them is so cheap, and they do all of this work

What do you mean 'free the slave?'
That could never be.
No way I could hire a man ,who looks just like me;
To do all of this work? And to do it all for free?
Besides, I can write and read.
There's got to be a way they'll stay
For this cause I'd die.
Come on y'all, let's rally together, and give a war cry.

We lick our wounds in the dust, but we're not dead yet.
I fear for my life; These men might rebel on us.
Never needed them before, so jails won't be enough
Lets make them 100 times bigger!
The federal government will support us.
We all need protection! And my women need safety.
Hey architects and engineers there's money here that we all could
Be making.
70 years later. The plantations are no longer in the South.
The North picked up when the factories died down.
The prison capitol of the world is Michigan
And the lives it mainly swallows is children!
Get them all off the street, criminals don't need rehabilitation:
You beat your wife and it's a covered up mistake
I yell at mine and it's a trip for me to go upstate.
On both accounts it's wrong, but whose punishment is right?
You drive your car drunk and it's a hushed probation; Get those
News crews out of here.

This is a judge of this nation!
I drive my car drunk and it's years behind bars I'm facing: 'Call the
Lansing State Journal to get this bum on the news.'
How many Judges are Black, Mexican or Indian?
How many prominent lawyers are Native American?
Who controls the judicial system?
Who even knows their rights?
How come so many injustices are swept under the rug
And some are shone under such bright light?

I'M A REPORTER

Find me on the inside, like Connie Chung and Dan Rather
My journey takes me behind enemy lines, where I beg to get free.
Only want to mingle with the population,
But I'm told my stay alone is best for me.
This close to the enemy; I never planned to be,
I can only do my best, While behind these walls is me.
To report back to the world
So that they know the reality of what's going on.
Inside of the Michigan prison industry,
The fighting in here that I see is all done wrong.
Instead of a unified front,
These criminals won't unite as won.
The plan of the captors is to keep them blind, deaf and dumb!
Keep the heads in isolation, so they won't rally the bodies along.
You heard about the one that did 25 years?
And didn't even kill no one!
Paid 11 million for restitution;
How does that compensate for 25 years of lost freedom?
This big business wants to shut us all up;
Send us away with our tails between our legs.
Quietly, I find myself on the inside. Ready to speak up:
Imagine if Rosa Parks never said nothing;
If Martin Luther King did not act when he did.
How much trouble would our world really be in!
We are again sliding into a cement grave
This cotton gin has laid claim to so many of our kids.
Who dares attempt to save our lost souls?
Inside this concrete hell so many so chose to play
But what's my life worth to God?
If for Him,
I won't enter into hell to help others find the way.
Like Iraq, I'm on the inside,
Willing to make some change.
I write these diaries to the world,
Knowing I'll be back home one day.
To publically publish these heroic works to the world

I pray everyday for my daughter;
I know this hurts.
Daddy's special mission is only at the beginning stages
God needs me to do much more work inside of these cages;
To find out what's really in here!
Know that I love you and God is your one and only
True father.
You'll understand later;
For now! Don't even bother

THE ACCUMULATION OF WEALTH

Gold, silver, brass and fold!
Those all mean nothing in comparison to the knowledge that
I know;
God put it here, but I'd like to see you
Try and take what I have gained with you!
When He puts His hand down to come and get you,
From this heaven to the next we give it all away;
Naked you came into this world, naked you shall leave your stay.
Once time stops, your work on earth will be no more
Will you come right in? Or be the one outside?
Knocking on heaven's door?
From this life to the next, we don't know what will be in store
My accumulation of wealth takes me well beyond the ocean floor.
Up through the moon, to infinity and beyond.
My brain is no longer human, it has transformed beyond eons.
Into a oneness with the divine;
Through my guide I am a divine being.
Each morning when I wake up,
He allots me another chance to be in the Kingdom.
Filling God's world of being with greatness,
Through these feeble hands of mine.
Being is my true accumulation of wealth;
The soul is divine.

TRYING TO MIX THESE WORLDS

Tell me what I was doing: trying to bring this union together.
We'll always be different; Like opposite polarities in stormy
Weather.
My summer is your winter,
And my day your night.
You say it was all for the love of my daughter, that I tried to do this right!
God brings understanding to the heart, in order to reveal His plan.
What we want is never so important,
When we look back on Her plan.
She sees the pieces all put together;
When we have no idea how they will fit.
Our differences are rooted from spiritual backgrounds:
Black is one with him; White is capitalist!
How much of it can you store away? When people really need it?
That poor man on the street, who cares if he really needs it?
No thought of his children at no-home, wife stricken with cancer.
Who judges based on outside appearance?
The Lord checks the inside pump to distinguish character.
I'd give my last dollar to a stranger in need.
Your reply would be, 'what about me.'
I've done my studies, infiltrating many cultures of the world!
Who told me to put mixed descent into my first born seed?
Will she be confused by this world,
Wondering where does she fit in?
It doesn't matter how long daddy is away
She'll always be my best friend.

HAVE YOU EVER SPENT TIME ALONE WITH GOD?

Have you ever spent time alone with Him
To embrace your inward parts?
Not saying a word as She touches, from your head to your heart.
No need for rationalization, because She already knows the truth.
Put down your pride and envy, and allow Her love to pour through.
We go to a doctor for an examination
And expect that he can tell us all.
Instead of going to the Creator, when He really knows it all.
From the inside to the outside, He know's the inner workings;
Why with this American made car? Would I go get it fixed in turkey?
How do we expect to hear the Creator talk,
When we can't even clear our mind?
How do you keep yourself busy,
When you have so much idle time?
The mind is like a radio;
If you're not properly tuned in you won't catch the right station.
The world is but a distraction, looking to distract our destination.
To find the spirit, you have to dig deep;
The dexterity is false.
No matter how deep you go; You could never touch the floor
Of the soul.
That's a camera you have to entrust to Dr. God;
Some places only He can probe.
Do you find yourself afraid to tell Him?
Thinking because She is not here that She does not already know.
God can hear all. Who implanted these senses into us all?
A biological surgery too advanced for man.
I look to the sky and repeat to myself, "I know He can, I know He can."
Please take my soul on a journey, to places I've never been before.
My mind is all locked up
And only you have the keys to open these doors.
I sit down and quiet the self;
Allowing of myself, for you to explore.
The more I listen to your teachings ,
The more I yearn to know more.
All credit due to the almighty
You are love.
In my time alone
My eyes stayed fixed
On you up above.

I AM THE FATE OF AMERICA

Point the finger at mista Obama if you like
He's only cleaning up the screw ups from 2002.
Now after one year in office, what did you really expect he could do?
Live up to his slogan,
And wave the banner of hope.
This ship was already going down;
In it, Mr. Bush put all these holes:
Rising gas prices; no health care for the needy;
The rich get rich,
For why are American ways always so greedy!
An instant drop in gas prices, and health care for all.
A re-distribution of the wealth,
Opportunity to rebalance the funds to us all.
Hope for the young, and life to single parent moms.
Even to the white house, bring back the belief in God.
Reform this crooked American dream,
And it all starts with all of us.
Blame it on the government, but the key in this here is us
I once heard when bad men combine
The good must also link up!
Why was I a State Trooper, now sitting in this jail all twisted up.
So much unanswered ink?
Guilty until proven innocent is the way it should read.
The media immediately took this case,
Now society wants the prosecution to slam me.
Faith in God is what keeps me alive!
Thank you Jesus Christ; Each day I die.
Even Jesus Christ was hit,
And they spit in His eyes!
His only reason to come here
Was to link us back to life.
Discovering the will of God,
Knowing that it lives inside the human race
Worldly wisdom is what kills us.
The devil is a lie against God's way
We know the world is the devil's playground
So why do we live by its systems?
I am the fate of America, just look in the mirror

TOO MUCH FIGHT

You expect me to quit?
Well you don't know Jesus too well.
My body is the temple
Inside of me is where the true God dwells.
Known for creating miracles,
Through those that believe.
I am of the few:
Take a long look into me.
Analyze my spirit and only God you'll extract.
You expect me to quit!
Should have known God better than that.

I AM A BRIDGE

Locked up or free?
Black or White;
Good or evil,
Death or life?

Ocean floor or galaxies?
Heaven from hell!
The ground floor and the atmosphere;
Where will you dwell:

Mind or body;
The heart or the soul?
Head or the feet;
Which way should we go?

The world or eternal life:
Wrong or right?
Innocent and guilty?
Day and night!

The New Testament or the old one?
Ending or the beginning;
I am the alpha and omega,
It's all in me just keep listening

THE LORD'S CRY FOR HELP

In this foolish world of earthly treasures
Why don't we realize the kingdom of heaven is forever?

Brother can you spare a dime?
I ain't got it.
Jesus is the one asking for it, and he knows you have it.

Wait till it's time to go to heaven and your names are not in
That book.
On your way back down, you'll have much time to take a second
Look.
Back on the possibilities of your life, to see the things
You could have done for others. Yet you chose not to proceed,
Stashing away earthly possessions from others.

Brother can you spare a dime?
I ain't got it
Jesus is the one asking and he knows you have it. Why lie?

How can we expect this world to change for the better
If we're not willing to change ourselves?
How can I have it right here in my pocket, and not give the less
Fortunate some help?
Hope in the form of a coin, but in our world we covet it all from
Fellow man.
The 200,000 dollars that you make this year
Is enough to build a plan.
The value of a dollar,
Is it more important than the Lord's spiritual plan?
If you really wanted it you could have asked
You didn't have to murder an innocent man!
A soul gone to heaven, and a life gone to jail.
That's what the devil calls a two for one deal;
Getting all of God's kids off his playing field.
This world, that we live in, is so greedy and corrupt.
When bad people form together for evil,
The good must also click up!
I sit in a cell, calling on the leaders of the world for help.
I never took anything from anyone, just want to go raise my
Baby girls to be their best.

119

The whole world turned its head saying,
'It's not my problem.'
Have you looked in that bible and read?
In Jesus steps, I'm following.
On a quest to become more like Christ.
Waiting for God to bring me to righteousness again;

Brother can you spare a dime?
I ain't got it
Jesus is the one asking and he knows you got it.

TO MAKE THIS GOOD

From difficulties to triumphs we turn the pages with faith.
With greatness comes challenges, longsuffering saves the day!
This worldly way was even difficult for Jesus
His soul paved the way.
Left us here as a mighty redeemer; our roadmap to show us
The correct way.
Here to help us through the dark day!
Everything works for good in the kingdom of God
For those who are believers.
Daniel's friends went through a mighty furnace,
And in with them was Son of God.
Went in bound, but came out loosed of soul.
Sometimes the path we want to travel is not the way God needs
Us to go!
How many will stay positive?
When He redirects your world in the blinking of an eye?
A bad situation will be positive;
We shall overcome...If we try.
The revolution from slavery was scary,
But through it my freedom has come.
A fall from a horse,
Brings a new movement for the paralyzed one;
From in a wheel chair your whole life, to walking again!
Miracles in the making
All orchestrated through the fate of man
The devil wants you to give in; not even try.
For you to quit is the only way evil will kill life.
How could you loose a battle that has already been won?
Father, Son, and the Holy Spirit, are my rising son.
From this world to the next, the victory is already done!
Faith is all we have to abide by;
After the darkness, will come the son.

To Break Free:

WHAT LIFE IS ALL ABOUT

About 3 foot 5.
Big brown eyes,
Long dark hair
                    I see heaven
                    Each time I
            Stare into your eyes!
                                    Wishing I were there.
                            Praying you'll never be here.
                                    In my dreams I can
                                    Hear your laughter,

Giggling in my ear.
Though your soul
Is so far away,
I still feel you so near.
                        Have faith my little
                    Angel, daddy will again
                        Hold you dear;
            Near to my heart, perfect unison once again.
                                    Hoping to re-create
                                    A spark! Never be angry
                                    With God. It's my fault
                                    That we're apart.

The day will come.
When we will get a
Fresh new start!
                Know that you will always be imprinted in my heart.

I HATE THIS PLACE

I know that love conquers all, but I hate it here.
God knows best; I'm not supposed to be in here.
Home with my family being a father to my daughter
Instead, I sit in this cell all day, well 23 hours!
Should have closed my mouth and waited for counsel.
I tried to help the police, now I suffer the consequences.
Family trying to get me home, knowing I don't deserve to be.
I've been a good man all of my life, now look at me.
Calling on the Lord, while my Saints stand aside; No help to me.
Many apostles have been to prison before
How about I give it a try.
Sending letters all across the world,
And can't get a pastor to come by.
Just hoping you could come and pray with me,
Help me to keep the faith.
I didn't even commence this crime,
But this home is where I now reside!
You should take the time to get to know me.
11 years or 5 it's all too much
Till free, I can count down my release date, one bag of coffee at a time.
But if God summons me to be;
So what!
Do we continue to fight and believe or just give up?

WHO IT REALLY HURTS

Send me to jail. It doesn't really bother me
You take the hit, in this messed up economy.
Sorry to my family; Who's going to pay the rent?
Time to collect food stamps. After bills, all the monies spent.
What a honeymoon with my wife; me draped in stripes.
We've lost two cars already.
Material wealth is nothing in the next life.
Judged by a judicial system that doesn't even believe in prayer.
This is the devil's playground; like Peter,
I'm an innocent man in jail.
My apologies to 2103. I refused to act.
Thought I was preserving lives.
Do you believe I should go to prison for that?
While I'm gone away who'll tend to my farm?
Guess we'll just jack up your taxes,
To pay for me to be behind bars.
My happy and energetic daughter!
The judicial system should be forced to take a look into her eyes.
Explain to her why daddy's going away
At night when she cries!
She's been joined to my hip for all of her life
Who really takes the majority of the pain
When you send good folks goodbye?

Love never dies
It only grows by what it's fed on.
Although we're many miles apart
Your love is what I'm fed on!
Keeping me nourished, within each molecule of my soul!
Your love is the afterthought that comes before.
The beginning and the ending of the waking me.
Until our bodies are again one entity;
My heart keeps breaking, not allowing me to sleep.
They thought this love was history in the making.
Groundbreaking! Is what you are to me
Each time you kiss my lips you touch the soul of me;
Weak knees with only the anticipation!
You are my one and only valentine;
Your love is amazing.
Even though the world has taken us apart
Our love will never die.
Just takes the spark
For an implosion that will never depart.

GLORY REVEALED

Through patience and longsuffering,
When all externals are stacked against thee.
Hold fast to the redemption of Christ
The Divine One's only son is now me.
Shamed by the world when He bore no sin;
Left us in the world, to live just like Him.
How many would sell God's soul after 40 days of temptation?
I wouldn't sell God out
Even when they said 20 years
For each of the three charges I was facing.
Each day and each night; on my knees I'm praying
Got introduced to the Metu Neter now my soul is racing.
Spiritually ascending, into the sky, out of the mist of sin.
The soul is dead to all these negative forces;
There is only the God left within.
This body is only a tent
Temporary housing until the time I go home to be with Him
Tell God thanks for the time we spend,
Now it's time to go eat fruit with my kids.
A rainbow of the spiritual ladder handed down in this world,
Inherited to your children;
Teaching spiritually through the western world.
A modern day apostle, Yes I Am He.
No one choose to stand up, but you can count on me.

THE POSITIVE THINKER SEES THE INVISIBLE, FEELS THE
INTANGIBLE, AND ACHIEVES THE IMPOSSIBLE.

WINSTON CHURCHILL

Once my body lie down, my soul comes to life:

The spiritual departs from the physical as the moon begins to cast its light.

My soul is on a mission, as my body desires to be free. My spirit is out of this place, going where it wants to be: home with my wife; to the park with my kids; at a high school play; college graduation; in church with my family; enjoying Sunday dinner; in heaven with my grandmother; having conversation with the spiritual leaders, on a quest to know more; performing live at the BET awards; Conversations with Beyoncé and Jay; My wife's face on our first big day; spending time walking with God, or floating down a lazy river; I am a farmer watching as this seed begins to mature, giving way to the harvest; swimming to another part of the world; in my spiritual world, there are no bounds to me. The possibilities are endless, God made me with this belief.

When my soul re-enters my body and once again I am awake. Back to my prison! I'm confused: Which world is real and which is the one that I create?

BIRDS FLOCK TOGETHER

Law abiding citizen; headed to prison.
Birds of a feather flock together.
Do you see the juxtaposition in this?
Where's the reformation? No restoration in this.
What's the ultimate plan for all of these felons?
Release us with the citizens? The prison creates better criminals
I've already attended four years of college;
Now let's go and check out the penitentiary.
Reformation of the mind is caused by renewing of the spirit!
I find myself headed to prison and God knows who did this.
I pray for you all, but you won't change me by this;
I'm a slave of Jesus Christ even If I sit in jail till 2066.
God walks with me, and Jesus is my brother,
We got the same Dad, just different mothers;
Although they are similar in that, they both watched us suffer.
Wanted to do their best to help, but God's plan is unavoidable.
I Am Christ; He lives in me!
I Am God; like a drop of water out of the sea.
This world is the devil's playground;
His seeds all surround me.
By God's word I won't be strangled or suffocated,
The angels will be here to harvest me.
My soul is starving you see, so I attract the word.
I don't apologize to the world!
But I'm sorry to my wife and girls.

ENERGY

Positive momentum; see it moving forward?
Although I'm in this negative situation
Evil still won't steal my joy from this.
Feel the evil all around, as I'm trapped inside this dark box
I feel claustrophobic, with no keys to these locks.
Know that one situation will change the whole world;
I use negative energy, to put faith in the young boys and girls.
Know that I'm larger than this environment
When filled with the power of Christ's blood.
I'm apologetic for the pain that I've caused.
I pay the price with my daughters' love;
Leaving them exposed
To the evils in this world;
Should be at home teaching them wrong and right.
God knows the outcome, but my decision has changed our worlds.
Now I sit stagnant with this momentum,
Begging for a way to release it.
If it's Gods will I'll sign a book deal
To dispense the million little pieces.
Knowledge across the world, but all the monies for you!
I give away all these riches,
Royalties for the world all given unto you.
The future still looks bright for both of my girls:
Innocent pearls; and I protect them as a clam.
I am but a ball of energy don't call me a man.

Heat, soap, and food somehow this has to come through.
I just used the bathroom could you please hand me some tissue?
This blanket, sheets and pillowcase, laundry bag and more.
Someone has to pay for these
Even after all the cutbacks and more.
How many have lost their job?
What will they do without the steady stream of pay?
I paid real good taxes, before my job was taken away.
Do you think about that when you come to work each day?
I hope you like your job, and that you put some stock money away.
Your pension plan is taking care of me
Thank Bush for that.
I know I made a mistake; I take accountability for that.
I consider myself not a prisoner to that:
I know I'm a slave to Jesus Christ.
Michigan has the most prisons of any state;
If you build them they'll provide!
How about we build more institutions to educate!
After school programs that teach life?
Teach the soul about the tree of life; A guide map to do right.
Show us and know they'll climb it with the great I AM.
Who pays the heat bill in here?
If it's so hot in here how about we turn on the fan.

RAW DEAL

Looking around this place, I see so many faces that resemble me.
Yeah, your shallowness goes straight to facial features
And skin tone,
But deep down God is in the likeness of me; and I Am She.
This world is the devil's playground.
So many saints end up locked down
While the devil's children out there freely running around.
In here we sit, waiting for Jesus;
The saints outside can't even plead for us.
Stick together sheep, or we'll all be swallowed one by one.
The strength is in numbers,
So why in so many different directions do we run?
Too fearful of the wolf when to stick together is our only hope;
"Oh ye of little faith."
God told us we are gods! Just open up the psalms and read.
When you open up the spirit and become enlightened
Just holler at me.
I'll be over here amongst this evil; a sheep amongst the wolves!
Like Saint Michael, I'll battle all the way up to revelations for his goods.
Through the New Testament and Old Testament books.
God is my creator, and He's given me the right to fight!
We have the power to slay all these devils, but in your mind
Lies your true favor.
Through time, there's only been one quite like me.
I am Ausar! Only to God and Jesus will I bow down on both knees;
Head to the floor, prostrate heart. You lost Saints follow me!
I fight this battle of spiritual warfare
For the God that is in me
This heart aint going nowhere,
Although i take the raw deal.

GOD IS MY REHABILITATION

Learning the spiritual levels, believing that I Am Jesus.
He created thee in his likeness, so yes, I Am He.
Some day we must realize that yes, we are gods.
Once again I am but a drop, and his blood is my pond.
If I take a cup to drink from the gallon, is it not the same thing?
If I take a shot from the bottle
Does it not have the same ingredients?
If I take a chip from the bag, will it not be in the likeness to the rest?
I speak to you as Jesus in parables.
Hoping you'll decipher this text;
Pass this test!
How many of us see ourselves the wrong way?
Looking from the dark side of the tree,
Never learning the correct way.
I am an Ausar man. There's not many like me.
Like Jesus, a rare breed. Left here to save the world, but this is
The devil's playground and his people rule in this kingdom.
Sitting in positions of all high places.
It's a wonder this world is so lost.
The anti-Christ have been planted amongst us.
Don't blame this on Obama.
Throw all the saints in prison if you want to;
We still going to heaven.
I laugh with you later when the prisons are empty and the world
Is filled come the day of rapture.
No matter where they are, God will come for His;
The Holy Angel extending a sickle through the clouds,
And the harvesting begins.
Get on your knees, no matter where you are.
Surrender your life to God
And give all the glory to the morning star.

JUST HERE TO DEFY THE ODDS

Put me away, and tell me I can't do it.
I delight in persecutions; I know God will pull me through it.
Left me in here to be an example to the followers
Only wanted to be a great father;
It's a bigger picture God wants me to show the world
With sorrow, why bother?
Watch how bright His beacon shines
All through this dark place.
When it's time to depart
I'll ascend as Jesus right in front of your face.

YOUR DIVINE LIGHT

I can see it shining through, although you're in such a dark place
The holy stench is coming off of you
Kind of like mace.
Stinging the eyes of unbelievers
Bringing hope to underachievers.
You're in hell to do missionary work,
Chains tied onto demons.
Spiritually; You're becoming enlightened, by the Metu Neter
My heaven is full of blessings!
I know because I set them there.
Stored in my Father's house by the promise of His letters.
That's something you can't talk about,
Because you've probably never heard.
Take time each day, to harvest seeds with Jesus and the word;
I know that She believes, but it is we that don't believe in us?
The human power of the soul. Is kindled by the Godliness deep within us.
Since She's filled you with a flame of holiness
Go ahead and start a blaze.
Let the Holy Spirit burn, till flames exude from your brain;
Feet like bronze and hair charred because of it.
Your divine light is something the world needs to see
You are filled with the holy seed;
That means God lives in the soul of us.

I HAVE JOY

Even when I'm angry, I'll never be sad.
My heart is filled with goodness and for that I'm glad
Thank you Heavenly Father, for inhabiting my soul.
Thank you Holy Spirit, for guiding me the way God wants me to go.
Thank you Jesus, for walking with me.
If the divine would not have sent you back, where would we be?
All lost in the New World without a shepherd to lead.
Thank you! I am an Ausar man.
I Am He

It's my responsibility to teach the others, the best I can.
My salvation was paid at a price
So each day I'm grateful for this new chance.
I have faith once my studies are done
You'll send me home as a bright light!
Could never forget about the kids you've blessed unto me.
In you they will take flight.

Never wait until the end result to be happy.
Fill your heart with joy right now. The present encaptures thee.
No production is made through frustration;
Turn that frown upside down.
In the pit of the abyss, even a deer is a bear;
The darkness of night will make a jackal of a hare.
Why do we throw the innocent to the wolves
And expect them not to become the night?
These prisons are filled with darkness,
Trying to stomp out our lights.

YOU LOOK JUST LIKE YOUR DADDY

Dark skin, brown eyes, thick lips just like mine.
Pale skin, slanty eyes, thin lips and nose.
Bronze skin, wide eyed, and pointed nose.
Dark skin, stringy hair
You are the Father to all of those.

THIS DARK PLACE

All around me is filled with darkness,
And I'm beginning to suffocate. I can't breathe a lick in here,
Plus it's damp and wet in this place.
Toss me in this dungeon.
I know I'm filled with God's light.
All of y'all look for Him on the outside;
I'm in continual prayer for y'all.
Hear the howl of the wolves and the slither of these snakes at night.
The rest have been invaded,
But my cell they won't overtake by freight.
You have filled thine molecules with goodness;
They burst, releasing faith.
Allowing the lost to be attracted to me,
And the dark to run afraid.
Fearful of my King.
Influenced by His bright light

WHERE'S MY HEAD?

Five, six, seven, eight, nine or ten?

Whatever y'all feel I deserve. Know that this is not the end.
God is my best friend; I identify with Jesus's word
I don't really know the meaning of this,
But I know there is a reason.
Tell me what you want, but my spirit; I'm at peace with it.
Make me do these years cause I'm through shedding tears for this.
Do me a favor and send the stacks back to my wife and kids
I know the word has messages so I read till I am in agreement
With it.
Knowledge is my nourishment,
Cause She told me there's a key in it.
I live God's life with passion!
Until He invokes this soul to again be with him.
No longer in this body. I meditate till I can again be with Them.
Yeah I had that shottie. Maybe there was a reason I decided to
Leave with it.
I could have taken those lives, but would God have allowed me
To be with him?
I could have taken those souls, but would I have ever been able
To sleep again?
Right now, to be away from my family sucks,
But in my dreams I can be with them!
Nightmares could have taken over my life,
But like Toni Braxton, I can breathe again.
He will avenge.
Revenge is just a tool of evil.
I only dream to be again
Once this pounding in my head stop protruding

Massive snow falls, major earthquakes in Haiti.
Mudslides in California! The births are now missing the babies.
Take a journey into Matthew, and study what is promised when
She cums.
All the signs are right in front of our eyes
The beginnings of Sorrows is almost done.
Then! Comes the saint's tribulations
After which, immediately the Son of God will come.
Pastor keeps telling me the rapture will be in his lifetime.
In case She's right, I heed the warning and step into my right mind.
Attempting to teach His people so none of them will be left behind.
People all decoyed by finance; spiritually deaf and blind.
All of this will be left behind when those angels begin to blow.
Who'll still be here to hear the trumpets blow?
Who'll be in the next world waiting at the door?
All of you that are taking your time better get ready.
This is hell on earth!
When God cums you better be ready.

I SPEAK FOR GOD

Call me crazy, but I find all my truth in His word.
Come back and look around; apply it to this world.
What is it really going to take, for you to open your eyes and see?
My innocence allowed me a prison term; the King has revealed
On through me.
Open the pages of His book, and blow the dust off His word.
I re-cite the parable of the fig tree, and you say that I'm absurd.
Well wither away! For refusing to bear fruit.
The choice is yours,
You decide what to do.
In my 28 years of life, I Am that book! I've eaten so much of the
Word! I Am that book
Not something you read once, but a lifetime of continual
Reflection on each and every word!
One-thousand two hundred and eighteen pages;
I now read that in one sitting and still get understanding.
Keep yourself prepared. You don't know when She's coming.
Will your lamp be void of oil when the Son makes his next homecoming?
You're a servant, and it's due season, who are you out there
Feeding?
If the Son of God is coming at an hour you do not expect
What is the consensus? Will you be in heaven or will you be left behind?
Still holding conversation with a person, that has already died.
You scratch your head in amazement, 'how did you just
disappear? Where did you go? And why am I still here!'
Nothing to be left, but a heaping pile of clothes; glasses and an
Earplug that was turned down low.
Listen to these words as I speak them through Jesus.
I am God who lives in me; this temple She leaves to me.
Its walls filled with God's word.
So here lies the true gold.
Diamonds all encrusted,
Glimmering in the word.

THE CHOICE TO BE EXCELLENT BEGINS WITH ALIGNING
YOUR THOUGHTS AND WORDS WITH THE INTENTION TO
REQUIRE MORE FROM YOURSELF.

OPRAH WINFREY

HE SENT ME

Many have been called, but only the few were chosen,
Who volunteers to do the dirty work?
No one wants to clean up all of these soiled clothing.
Even Jesus was looked down upon because he dwelt among
The heathens.
Who truly needs the healing? The healthy,
Or the ones living with the sickness?
I am a doctor in this infirmary, in an attempt to heal some children.
The masses have all lost faith.
I am a motivational speaker.
Faith without works is dead, works without faith is naught.
God controls these hands and feet; To him I am a robot.
Knowing that She holds the controls; by the word I Am on auto pilot.
I find this soul in a place many dare not desire
In here it's hard to keep the faith,
When darkness is everywhere you go.
He sends messages through the soul consulting me to stay low
Only then is He strong! And it is He who carries me.
He has sent me to the depths of hell
Her love keeps upholding me.
"Don't be afraid, only believe." (Mark 5:36)
Though we walk through the valley of death you provide me
This strength.
Want to or not,
I Am sent to hell!

GAINING SPIRITUAL WAIT

My worldly weight is down
To see me you'd think I was stressed
Yet my spiritual weight is obese,
Just look at this heart inside of my chest.
My chest is lighter than a feather
After all this I can still sleep.
The devil came at me with an awful attack; didn't you think
You could kill Jesus?
I was told this is an evil world, so I plan for them to go your way
This soul will keep on fighting, with these present day saints
Until Jesus comes back to lead the way;
Like Mel Gibson in Braveheart, or the movie 300;
My faith wont waiver one bit though the odds stacked against
Me seem insurmountable.
Come get me if you can. My being's protected by the all
Powerful plan.
From this world to the next. It's all going as planned.
Open up your eyes before it's too late to wake!
I'm glad God separated me so I could study and wait.
Sharing the fruit with my children. It is God's power that did this.
The devil tried to take me away, but God's goodness will always
Reign through this.
For those who are called to good according to his purpose
Gaining spiritual weight is our only purpose.

THEY GOT THE RIGHT LIGHT

Watch it light up this cell; These inmates can't sleep at night.
She floods me with so much light,
This whole block is too bright!
Sneaking into the hallway, by the cracks under the door.
It's not too long before Her light touches, this whole second floor.
Splitting in the stairwell like molecules and atoms.
Half descends, while the other half ascends; darkness is what
It is after.
Continuing this well planned attack,
Invading the first and creeping onto the third floor.
On this darkness, it sheds light.
Floor by floor and door by door.
You expect darkness to breed here;
Well I'm here to shine some light.
Goodness will prevail; Illuminating the lunar, even at night.
This brightness even touches the keepers;
Sentenced to more time than me:
Many of them are 50 and they've been here since the age of 23.
Hoping to retire, long before they ever get fired.
Beds are opening up all over the place,
Even prisons' monies are declining.
There's change happening all over the land
Open up to Matthew 24;
God wants us to save as many as we can.
What good is that money? Or your house? Even your family
Vehicles can't save man. What will you do when the rapture begins?
Pay your way into heaven!
Stay here for those next seven years?
For what you'll witness! You'll need all that you can have down here.
If I have to stay here too! I'll survive.
If that's what God needed me to do.
If you're lost to what I'm talking about. I suggest you pick up
A bible and pursue it.
Undo me so we can all be more like Them?
He is my hero; the saving grace for all of humanity.
The qualities She exudes are those that I demand.
Thanksgiving to Her for giving man the power of He!
You don't know how to use yours?
Read about that mustard seed.
Faith will move mountains, but so many of us haven't found it.

Thanks to it, my faith has moved many many of mountains;
Heaps and piles of evil all coming for me.
The Word already told us
That we can get through any adversity.
Just another showing for the Supreme Being
To unfold its glory.
If you have no faith now,
I hate to see you at the ending of this story.
For many a new beginning, for others a sure ending.
I suggest you get down on your knees and repent.
Jesus is the only bridge and one of the bricks is me
My only job in this world, is to take you back with me.
Tempered by the fire, till only God's reflection is left.
Look me in the eye and tell me, this isn't Jesus pain that I reflect
Being gave us the power. We can be as Him.
These laws are of the new.
Not the old
Think spiritually,
Not of men.
Elevate your mind set. You're a divine being not a human.
Levitate thy self,
And this whole place will be illuminated.

STILL INSPIRED

Tell my daughter I miss her.
Tell my mother I love her,
My sister's the best.
Mad love for my brother.
Tell my father I'll be home soon, this isn't the end of this.
Yeah I been sentenced, but I'm making the best with it!
Know this is not the end.
God is my only juror; This courtroom's all tainted,
Influenced by on lookers.
I am God, please do me like they did to Jesus!
This is the last step, left for me to be as Jesus;
Tell all my people in the courtroom to dry your eyes.
I am a sacrifice, which means with God I will again rise.
You hoped that this would kill me, but know that this is not the end.
I'll go and sit away, to spend more time alone with Him.
My being wants to be a motivational speaker; what will I do
When life gets hard?
No time to turn away. Got to stay strong for my family beyond these bars.
Throw us in this fire pit; And one more inside when you take a
Glance inside.
Coming out unbounded and uncharred by the fire.
Through faith in God best believe ill never give up on thee;
The devil is a liar.
Still inspired
Is the main downfall in me.
The spirit will always pick me up. Even after I crash into trees.

WE STILL GROW

Through these extreme situations, we still grow.
So much adversity like green plants growing in the snow
Find vegetation in my desert
Some firm ground in this swamp
This family surrounded by quicksand; still won't drown.
As strong as the wood of the shittah tree, just look at thee.
Grown under adverse circumstances in the desert; perfect for thee.
As Jesus to grow up a tender plant
As a root out of a dry ground!
The process is only to mature our temperament;
How many will drown?
Void in this cold world, lost in the world with no faith!
My being is otherworldly divine; Not of the human race.
This soul is alien. No it's not from here!
Only here to educate y'all, before again we must disappear.

MY HERO

I know you're very busy and might not even get the chance to
Read this!
My hope is in the future; you gave me reason to believe in this.
Even when the going is tough, you never give up on audacity.
Your spirit helped kindle a fire! Now I write for the world to
Unleash the passion held within me!
Courageous you are for choosing to stand in the fire!
Carrying the weight of a dark office
And vowing to bring light into it!
You are our voice of inspiration; just wanted that you know.
In the world that we live in, people can often be so cold.
Afraid to speak up! Not wanting to go against the masses.
You are halfway through a term;
How many more will it take to fix this disaster?
Everyone points the finger, but how many go out and do?
In the world that we live in
I wish there were more people like you!
Not afraid to try, or give hope a chance.
Have you ever tried to spell triumph without the word try in it!
I admire you for spreading hope, even in the times we fall;
Thomas Edison found 9,999,999 different ways how not to build
The light bulb!
You are my president!
I support you through trial and error.
If the people of this place are so perfect
Why can't they put this broken ass country back together?
With the snap of a finger, to end all hunger.
The twitch of a nose, to end unemployment.
I'm content with the state of your foreign affairs;
Continual prayer for you!
All faith that you will live your life, healthy and long;
Your wife and daughters too.
Don't claim to know you on the outside.
Neither have I met Dr. King
Like he, you changed the face of our society,
Gave us a reason to believe.
Not taking away from your mixture,
You are hope to us all.
No matter what happens through these next two years,
Continue to hold your head tall

153

06-13-10

Six and a half years is not enough time with God,
Give me thirteen!
The word tells me, 'If told to run a mile and a half, then run three."
Look at me; A soldier trained by God!
Mine enemies thought it was over when the State Police fired me.
Know that in my weakness He's back, stronger than ever before!
Still will be a role model to my family
Even If I never see my daughter again.
Like a hero or a legend!
Just a soul that never dies
A Black rose that grew from concrete.
See 2-pac through my eyes!
We will rise! And live on to see a brighter day.
Just keep your faith to the sky; Don't get caught up
In all the disarray.
This world is of evil, and it's to get progressively worse.
When the time comes do you dare to be apart of the 144
Thousand followers left after the Rapture?
Call me crazy if you want to
You better re-read that chapter!
John the Baptist seen things his eyes could not fathom.
The world thought Noah was a disaster;
God's Word he continually chattered.
Look at the signs all over, as footprints in the snow!
Oh the earth is trembling again!
I gotta go!

I AM NOT YOU

Why is it that you don't understand me?

Is it because I am God; evil of this world is not in me.
Dead to Sin
Is it my vast amount of prayer that offends you?
Maybe it's the meditation. Were you expecting Buddha?
My being has God's home number.
Get your spiritual game up!
My feet are bronze, fiery red eyes, hair of wool. Stand up!
You don't understand? Go seek John in Revelations!
Even Jesus was physically beat and laughed at, by the people
Who stood to benefit the most by the project He was undertaking.
I Am He! Take a look at what my community did to me!
Filled with deceit.
Still there's not a drop of hate in the heart of me
I pray to God for those prosecutors, and to the Judge,
That God comes into your hearts
And creates a spark!
Is it really that joyful for you to send my kids to prison?
Make sure they all have rap sheets,
Felons long before they ever even get to start living.
A life in tribulation, before it's even begun.
It's O.K. I know you need to save all the real jobs
For your own sons!
True wealth is in mental health and wisdom.
Finances are nothing; my mind can will it.
I know why you don't understand me;
I am a divine being and I rely on the inner spirit.

BLACK PEOPLE DON'T READ

Someone once told me that Black people don't read.
Then what am I cooking for, if my family don't plan to eat?
We've come a long way from the world of segregation.
We all have a chance in this favoritized nation.
Given a chance to unite the world if we never look back.
I read to reknow history, head forward. Understand that?
Our freedom is through literacy.
So give your education a chance.
Why are all my kids out to be the biggest dope men?
Only second hope is a rapper.
The rest an athlete want to be.
Where are my doctors? Lawyers? and judges at?
You coulda saved me!
The next goal is to become a minister; I can feed the people.
God told me to write it all down.
But how many Black people will read it?

GOT THE DEVIL OFF SCHEDULE

You are the master of deceit, but God knows all!
Listening to the good in life, Saints never fall;
Stand tall, although you offer the world.
This world is only temporary
The eternal kingdom is within another world
This world is just an illusion, to flatter lost souls
My house is up in heaven; with the Lord I must now go.
Content to dwell in the tent, while we do His work!
Never said this would be easy,
Told us it would hurt.
Like Jesus, we are only here to do your work.
I know these poetics won't sell, so I give them to the church!
The most important book in the world; what is it worth?
Given away for free! Who does it hurt?
The goal is not to make millions; It's to educate the people.
Do not riches follow, every love-based leader?
"Come to me." Allow me to teach you of the tree of life
Let's assess your spiritual level, and like Lazarus bring you back to life.
From the way of the world, to one with God.
My nature is in Her; She is I
I vow to be a God-man; I Am He
Got the devil off schedule
Because he can't bother me.

SORRY FOR BREAKING YOUR HEART

I see you crying, and I feel your tears.
It's all my fault. I'll have to go away for years;
Shoulda responded better. That's what I was trained for.
I was the one taught to be kicking down doors.
For a seizure of drugs, I know your ears are innocent.
There's no need to go into it too much, but you have to hear this:
Only for you to know the truth; I was also robbed.
I shoulda told the truth and thought more about you.
Sorry for breaking your heart how will I make this up to you?

To 2103 Cogswell. I humbly repent.
For the goodness of God, I know our paths will cross again.
Right now we are betwixed, by evil that the law won't let us
Pull apart.
There's a letter here for you, from the bottom of my heart!
I meditate that God will heal you
Remove your heavy heart.
Allow you to sleep again, when you here a thud in the dark.

My being won't allow me to give in, the world must know!
The fallen trooper still has dignity
Integrity won't turn cold!
I owe you my all. With exception of wife and kids.

I didn't do this directly, but indirectly I take responsibility for this.

GUIDE MY STEPS

With you as my feet! There's trust in these steps!
From one decision to the next, your love is why I Am blessed.
Bundled to this heart; ingrained in this mind.
Your word gives the direction, we must take in order to find;
The way to be in step with the soul.
Equal distribution for heart and mind
You left us with this Holy Spirit and unto it we must bind.
Until it has the reigns; The blind faith of us.
Your love and ability to take the first step, is what we must trust!
You see the big picture, long before we ever have the pieces.
If writing is what this soul must do in your world,
Then send me the pieces!
Thank you for supplying the ammunition
To load this spiritual gun.
The devil has been robbed of the victory,
For you have already won.
We know tribulations are near, still there's nothing to fear.
Your word supplies us with the strength we need, until you are
Once again near.
Keep illuminating this temple, and for you I'll light the world on fire.
My being only wants to give hope to all of these young boys and girls
Elders and seniors, help teach them the meaning,
Show them the need for the burning desire.
Open up this book, and we'll go through it word for word
To find its meaning, when so much just seems to have no meaning.

A REVOLUTIONARY

These poetics will change the world,
As they are inspired by the word.
Spirituality teaches us to directly talk to the spirit of love above.
Thank goodness for the New Testament,
And our life through Jesus Christ.
Even She doesn't do it alone; She has vessels in order to feed us.
Yet how do we tap into them? As spiritual unbelievers;
We're lost and can't find the breast for nourishment, from these
Willing leaders.
What are we to do? If our physical guides don't know how to
Lead us?
The oracles are steady. They are already pleading for us.
Long before we even know, that they are spiritually here with us
So many of our spirits have gone sour, and the world does not
Agree with us!
Send them all to prison! With no hope that they'll ever change!
If renewing of the mind is the transformation of the spirit,
Why don't prisoners meditate?
Mind all confused. How many can spend quiet time away?
Ingest the word. As if it is the only food I can take.
Find me here as a tour guide, as John to Patmos had to go,
I'm in hear doing my bidding:
My job is to be the scribe and take down all these notes.
On a mission like a soldier in Iraq, know that I pray for y'all to
Come home.
The enemy is within; America's beginning to fall alone.
Thank goodness for Barack. The Obamas are a pillar of family
To us all!
Even after, from the White house, they be long gone.

When my being, in this mission, is complete
That's how I aspire to be!
A great husband and father, leading my family to the well to drink.
Watching as they rejuvenate ; The spring goodness: removing all bother.
Worry has dissipated; The Divine Being is the true Father.
My field is growing. I can't wait to give the crop to the followers
Planted; these seeds day by day, each and every one!
The true joy is the harvest; watching it feed its people in the
Morning Son
Don't worry about me, I'm not ready yet to eat;
The temple's all dirty, and it still needs to be cleaned.

160

Polluted by the way of the world, don't only clean the outside
The true dwelling of this holy relic is what lies on the inside.

Spiritual revolutionary! Its hands crafted me to be
I am Ausar.
Can't you feel beings energy flowing through me!

PERPETUAL OPTIMISM IS A FORCE MULTIPLIER.

COLIN POWELL

THE VOICE IN MY HEAD

Firm, convincing, I feel you near.
How many times have I tried to shake you away?
Yet and still you're right here.
Guiding me to what's right, but now I think I know!
My way got me lost. Trampled out in the cold snow.
It's cold in this pit, and I can see no way out of it.
In despair, my being hands over the reigns to you,
And you drive us all right out of this. Me plus another two.
Why hadn't I listened to you before? So long ago.
Trusting in myself; What did I ever know from afore?
Needing help from someone else that knows.
You were given to me; A gift to come at a mighty cost.
The Supreme Being knew in this world, that we'd be lost.
We're left with Her voice to guide us,
Lead us in the correct way.
Your work is my lampstand
On you we will sit and wait.
Listening to your direction, before I go off on my own.
There's the reason, Jesus meditated and prayed so much alone:
He knew he was never alone!
As Moses and Daniel we also have you.
How do we slow down and listen?
Untill your station is well tuned?
Find us busy with the world, mind too cluttered to hear your way!
Thank you for changing my world, and sending me a whole
New way!
No longer distracted by the noise. That once pulled me away.
We are your children, it is you who has grounded our faith.
Post me as a rock
On this unstable ground
I know exactly whose voice that is leading me.
Now that My inner Holy Spirit has been found.
When I was down and out, you were my lost and found
Thank you for taking the time out to turn me around,
Leading me the correct way, loosed shall be our bounds.
Will still continue to make the world bright.
Once I leave this narrow way,
Jumping off into that bright light;
Doing exactly what your voice may say.

I'M NOT IN JAIL

Not a prisoner to this body, do what you must to me.
My mind is in a whole different space,
In God lies the trust of me.
I spend so much time alone with God;
I am amongst the stars.
Tell my family I'm sorry. I'll be home as soon as possible.
From this safe place, God allows me a harvest;
To be given all away, thank you for blessing me with this knowledge.
Wisdom and understanding, worth far more than gold.
The Holy Spirit illuminates these footsteps,
Showing me the correct way to go.
Even from this wicked place, a positive; God will show.
I thank goodness everyday, that you used this to save my soul,
Like Jesus, this life was lived at a cost.
Jesus is my brethren by the blood
God is who we worship in this house; Please fill us all up with love
You may call it prison religion, but just wait and see.
I'm so optimistic, these shoes don't even fit me.
No time to hold the head down,
Keep the chin to the sky.
My God has chastened me. No need to ask why.
Just spend time in this resort, and vow to never do it again.
I pray for my people in Haiti,
I know that this is not the end.
Your lives look to be rough right now
I pray for you every night.
That God touches you with His love,
I save the tears for you when I cry at night.
No time to complain of my tribulations
When compared to the troubles of you.
I cry myself to sleep at night
Asking God what more can I do?
Gods reply is to, 'keep gardening;'
He'll send fruit to me to give to you.
The media has attempted to make me an animal in my own home,
I invite you in for a cup of coffee and a honey bun too.
Take time to do an interview; and get to know the real me
Learn how much I give, see what you do to my family.
I am not in prison.
My mind is at home; I spend time in the temple with God
Waiting to physically get back home.

166

Thanks be to the gods that I spoke through,
We did this from jail.
There's only one high priestess that we proposed to
And She said yeah.
Even from in this place,
The goal was to never give up through whatever.
Through the spirit, rise from this with goodness,
Thank God above through whatever.
All praise to my Father, for being the support.
I left my wife at home to take care of all of the child support;
And she really showed up!
Took it all in stride.
Each victory helping us get through this, just one day at a time.
Thank you for filling my life with goodness
We'll always be like twine,
Now that we've finally made it
I'm glad you got that Q-7 truck in your life.
Never have to work again, just volunteer your time.
Do things for those in need, because that's what God's expecting.
All this money that we have is not for me or you.
Faith moves mountains, and we have stood tall in truth
Thank you God for this rock; our enemies wanted us to crawl.
Waiting for the fall of a lifetime when to trust in God is all.
You un-believers are so confused, don't know what to do.
Thank you to the world for purchasing this word
I wrote Oprah for months, but got not even a positive word.
Now that I'm refined, we stare down from the booklist.
Don't worry Oprah, I put myself onto your book list.
Sometime people just need a little pick me up when the devil
Is trying to seduce.
They all have cried out, but how many saints would answer if
The call was to you?
'That ain't my problem.' This disease spread like covid.
Sin is malignant; passing from one soul to the next victim.
Love is the only cure for it.
But away from it you go.

Jesus dwelt with the sinners; do you not get the connection?
Nothing is more important, than giving a lost soul new direction;
Find me embedded on the best sellers list.
Given this life over to God, so address me as Reverend Jones.
God positioned me on the National Bestsellers list,
I'm just an unknown scribe.
Still writing this all down.
Journalist behind enemy lines.
Writing down this situation, on whatever I can find.
Parch these words upon my soul.
The tongue to be so mighty;
Mine no more than yours.
"Will you ever sit at the top?"
Already there.
National bestselller list!
We already been there.

Ask the whole world, and they say I should fry.
Because I didn't tell the whole truth, or blatantly tell a lie?
What do you do? When your family's lives may be in danger?
Military weapons, held by perfect strangers.
What do you see when you look into my eyes?
Just another crooked cop, who deserves to die!
In God lies my refuse. The Father controls my life
Say what you want to, through God I'll never die.
Thank you to Jesus, this battle is already tried!
666 is the number, over my head you hung:
On my 6th day of fasting, you offer me a 6 and a half year deal.
Multiple that half by the date; Feb. 12th,
And what do we have here?
Now how is that tempting? Asking me to bow down
Give in to the math of three sixes!
On top of that you direct me to cooperate by lies and fear.
With men this is impossible, but through God all things are
Possible!
That's Matthew 19:26; one of Gods holy apostles.
Expect me to be angry. Well this soul's at peace
Even when it's blatantly evident the devil is after me.

SHE'S BACK

Yeah you went for a minute, gave some a scare.
I was right there with you spiritually
Though the world thought I wasn't there.
Knowing you were away with God, is the only way I got through
Meditating from Monday to Thursday
Knowing that when they pulled those tubes out you'd come to.
You are stronger than the world
My might when there is only weakness,
I've cried so many tears, I'm tired of weepin.
Faith tells me you're alright, just walking with God
You speak to him directly, then communicate with us all.
I know for the best! So there is no worst,
Faith will move mountains, but for you I hurt.
The devil is out to bother me; one soul at a time.
I wrote 'when you wake up to evil'
But I did not know exactly why.
Couldn't quite figure out why my hands kept moving,
If anyone would have told me that that would be your story
I would have just been through with it.
No matter what they told me;
Just wouldn't stop believing it.
Who could have informed me that my character would be you?
The great thing about it, is that she made it through.
I'll see you physically when you come from home
In the mean time, spiritually, I will continue to pray with you.

FAILURE

Through all the success in life,
God needed me to fall again.
Trip me and throw me down on my face;
Deliver me to the evil one by my own sin.
Not till I am completely weak, does She make me strong.
She is my reason for life;
Keeps me moving on.
Giving me a reason to hope; A belief in Her plan.
Moses was quick tempered, and had taken the life of man.
Abraham was a deceiver, and David murdered too
Still what exactly is it we remember,
Those biblical scholars for doing?
Failure is to test your faith,
Show God which way you will go.
In the meat of adversity, will you give up on what is foretold?
Open up your bible, and read the story of Job.
Never would he give up, no matter how bad his life seemed to go.
Never even said a mumbling word,
Wouldn't throw in the towel to blaspheme God
Know that I die daily, no matter how many times I fall
My faith is all in God, whether I'm free or in jail
The devil is a lie! Leave my family alone and go back to hell.
You can't have my mother, I know she'll be here again.
You see this as my failure.
But by hustle and belief I will win.

WELCOME

Knew you'd be coming back,
Though I won't be there to greet you when you get home.
We gon' celebrate!
The devil is a lie; thought he could ruin the reign of love.
Time spent with God, is the best time for all for us.
You are the likeness of Lazarus
On the 4th day you're to come home to us.
The family continued to grieve
I told them it was alright.
You are simply spending time with the Lord, Our Father is
Doing you right.
By faith I keep believing,
I'll see you in the nights
Just to call you on the phone, To hear your voice at night.
When it's time,
I keep believing, I'll be there to give you a hug.
No matter what they say,
Thank you Mom for everything
Welcome home, back to your space and our love.
Overjoyed God sent you back to us.
They told me this would never be;
Watching your gradbabies grow up.
God is the miracle worker,
By faith we welcome you back by belief.

GEARING UP FOR WAR

I find myself in a war. Much of the world wants me to lose.
I must choose my direction methodically;
Put God's word in my shoes.
Your letters shall be the lamps, to illuminate my paths forever
These prosecutors have no evidence against me.
My own mouth I blabbered.
Fearful for my family; my relatives with me too.
Don't want to fathom an end to their lives,
On the account of my bad choosing.
My apologies for lying to the detectives,
I was fearful of the outcome.
The criminals are the ones that got away.
You must convict someone!
Didn't know if my family was in danger.
I didn't know what else to do.
I'd kill myself for my families' safety
What would you do?
I am a living sacrifice. The jury will see me as the same.
I will get home to my wife and children,
And become State Police again.
I do live my life with integrity
Each and everyday.
I wish I woulda been a detective or a lawye, and I would
Have known exactlt what not to say.
This war is not over, till God takes me home.
Faith will light the way.
Thanks to God all my fear has gone.

HOW WE OUTSMART THE SYSTEM

The goal is to stick together
No matter how bad they try to trick us.
Keep faith in the almighty, even after they've tricked us.
From police to prosecutors what are we supposed to do?
You even wanted me to turn on my family
After I tried to help you, what did you do for me?
A brother-hood you call it
Well you fraternized against me.
Thank you Hugh
For being a real brother, and coming to save me!
You picked up the loose pieces, when they tried to pick me apart.
Gave me a new chance with my daughter,
For that there's no price I would not pay.
Money is useless in the spiritual world
You charge me 30 thousand and I'll tip you 30
When I get home and these books begin to float away!
God is the true judge.
The ruler of us all,
Make these feeble, weak knees, once again stand strong

I WON'T QUIT ON YOU

Don't quit on me!
I won't give up on you.
Even when we don't know which direction to go
And we're both all confused.
Many will decide to walk away
But through it all, I walk to you.
No matter how tough it gets, how lost and confused.
Even though I see no finish line in sight,
You won't let me loose.

THE MIND THAT SAYS I CAN

Knowing that it's never over
Until you voice, 'I quit.'
This world is only physical,
But it's the spiritual world that rules in it!
How do you tap in?
Know the value of, 'I can'?
Tell me what's impossible,
Knowing you've picked the right man.
With God all is possible, just take ahold
Fast to faith:
Jesus didn't come when Mary called;
Lazarus was already dead for four days.
All from no patience and lack of faith,
Jesus answered the call.
Even though he decided to wait,
Faith is what makes mountains fall.
Even when the masses fall,
The mind that says I can,
Will watch as all of the barriers
Turn into sand.

TOO BUSY PUTTING US AWAY

The world is all in chaos.
So many of us are lost.
Not sure of which way we need to go
Walking in circles like robots.
And those are our leaders, so what are we supposed to do?
Down here at the bottom, trying to get our families some food.
Even the innocent are found guilty, if they don't have money.
Those who have it are all too greedy, squeezing the wads down
Counted down to the lowest number.
God tells us to share all if we want to get into heaven.
This earthly run-down is nothing, just a simple testing.
The true riches lie in heaven.
All of which we store away
Through all of the persecutions and tribulations,
Keep that frown at bay.
The prosecutor wants to be a judge,
And the lawyer wants to prosecute
Police are out to get a raise,
So what are the people supposed to do?
Spirituality is the war-fare
The decoy is the Middle East.
I was offered 6 and one half years because I was the State Police!
Should have handled the end result better, but it's my family
Who suffers.
Now in this messed up economy,
There's one more single parent mother.

THANK YOU FOR GIVING ME THE REASON

Thank you for giving me the reason
It's all thanks to you that we shout.
From the jails of Lansing, MI
To the mountain tops of Mount Sinai
Scream out!
Let your voice be heard,
We thank you for the victory.
Never will we ever give up the faith
Even when evil thoughts get the best of me.
From this world to the next, we are formed by faith.
In the midst of the storm, Jesus only slept the winds away.
How many of us will patiently wait?
Allow him to get his rest, knowing it will all be O.K?
Because He is right here standing next to us,
We will live to see the next passing day.
Even when the world wants to deceive us
We don't go cower away.
Stand up strong like Jesus
Knowing God will lead the way.

CHOOSE THE POSITIVE. YOU HAVE A CHOICE. YOU ARE
THE MASTER OF YOUR ATTITUDE. CHOOSE THE POSITIVE,
THE CONSTRUCTIVE.

BRUCE LEE

CHAINED TO GOD

You call me an inmate, but I know I'm a soldier for my Lord.
A prisoner of God!
So yes I'm uncomfortable stuck behind these locked doors.
Suffering through this pain,
But I only see my mom:
Lying in that hospital bed; Spirit chained unto God.
I know that this body is only a tent.
Right now you are at home with God
I know with us again you'll roam.
It always takes so much, for us to value our human gifts..
To have you back here,
We can do a transplant;
You the lungs from my body,
I know one day you'll read this.
Just wipe away the tears
I never expected to see you so weak
You've been our strength for years.
I'll continually keep the belief,
Be it 14 days or 21 weeks.
Choosing to be gleeful, in each and every piece
You are chained to God spiritually,
Physically I lie here and wait, He paid the price for my life
Visa, Discover, American Express?
Priceless! Is the expression that says it best!
Here we are in a recession, and I'm thirty thousand again
No price is worth the amount to see my daughters
Beautiful smile again. Please spare my mothers' life!
I ask that you please bring her back.
Would hate to do time in prison,
But for her, the rest of my life you could take back.
Sorry to bring all of this trouble
On my friends and family.
I know I will do better.
2103 Cogswell street, I hope we'll grow to be friends later.
Allow me the opportunity to plead for my life
Know that my harvest grows
Only because of your cries.
Knowing that you're chained to God,
Wipe the tears from your eyes.

Mental anguish, material wealth can't pay
But this is all for you in hopes fo a better day.
Checks for restitution that could never cleanse the thumps n the night away.
Much was taken from you and I need you to know
The real thieves got away
At times I still wish I woulda shot and just ended their days.
All I could think about was all the houses on that block.
Thanks to Jesus blood and mercy no one got shot.
I learned a valuable lesson
More important than gold.
Refined by the fire
Now I hope you see
How Jesus face has grown upon me.
When you look at me, tell me what do you see?
Me burning my harvest
Laughing delirious in the heat.

Fire everywhere!
All that hard work from these feeble hands.
I don't have enough water to quench it, burnig all my lands.
Look now it withers my plants.
What can I do with it?
With help I would only flood my own grounds
Making it too hard to cultivate when the fire no longer exists.
Once the fire starts to drown,
I stand in the midst of it all
And watch it all burn down.
My wife and I watch as the kids sleep,
Yet there are more reflections amongst us;
Crying tears of joy, but not enough to stop the heat.
Faith and optimism tells me the ground will be fertile
After all this heat.
Ashes of burned vegetation to mix amongst
This dry ground.
Will form particles of nutrients
Once the reign begins to come down.

PLANNING THE OFFENSIVE

Hope and a dream is all that I have left.
Going to the masses, to help me out of this mess
Freedom will happen, but for the cost of a dollar
I'm sorry for how this happened
But this happened to learn better choices for tomorrow;
Souls were saved,
But now my physical self is put away.
All I know is that I will see my daughter again
In God's way.
No will to give up
You'll have to fight to put me away.
With God as my witness,
Jesus performed miracles everyday.
Listening to the voice of God
I wait for Her to tell me the correct way.
Move forward by faith
Knowing God will open up the way.

FIGHTING FOR MY DAUGHTER'S LIFE

Not giving up, but this aint about me.
I've got a creation at home that God has given onto me:
Light brown eyes, about 3'3"
Much prettier than I, but a recreation of me.
I made a promise to my heart, that I would never leave.
Six months later, now look at me.
Locked in this cage with faith for a day of release.
Why would I take the six and a half year "deal" that you're offering
Onto me?
Thanks to my nightmare team: Maddoloni and Grabel.
Mr. Clarke has came in off the bench
To earn most Valuable player.
One thing's for certain; Daddy's coming home.
We've got a lot of time to make up for
Daddy's on the way home.

I'M COMING HOME

Lawyer after lawyer,
Day after day
One way or another.
I've got to get out of this crooked place.
Stuck in this cage, for 23 hours per day!
Thank goodness I'm so close to God;
Through this, grew even closer to His ways.
Without you I woulda lost my way!
Thank goodness you sent the spirit of Jesus to lead the way.
Like Daniel I fought lions,
Woke up sweating in my sleep;
Awoke at trial,
And Goliath was the judge for me.
My mother is back here with us now.
devil tried to take away her love from me!
I knew that you wouldn't do it
To God I pleaded that you would again just be.
To come back into your tent; give you life again.
Not time for you to go to heaven yet,
Not with the world like this.
A more positive note, is what I pray and hope for in the end!
God is our comforter, so through all this we can still live.
Tell my daughters' I love them,
Thanks for being so patient.
Daddy's coming home!
Keep believing and we will make it.

EXHALE

I know the stress is getting tense; The heat in this fire is thick
I sit in here and meditate, with grace as my best friend.
How do I stay so cool; Knowing God will win!
He is in my soul and I Am in Him.
Take a deep breath, and let all of that heat out!
Jesus overcame the world
The word also flows through my mouth.
Speaking His words
As I Am in Him.
I love these trials and tribulations, that I Am currently in;
Allows me to draw Her within me.
Know that I'm given peace
Thank you that I am finally free;
To spend my lifetime chained unto the king.
Until I breathe my last;
Breath taken away,
And with that I smile.
Knowing that I died today.
Not only one time,
But each of these breaths could be my last.
Not promised these moments!
Live each as if it's my last.

Years of my daughters' lives, in the hands of counsel.
Who dares stand up for me, when this case looks to be impossible?
Already paid for those, who dare to put me away.
Asked for a second opinion, so we live on to fight a new day.
New aspirations, so now we got hope!
I don't question your ability to do
I only question the motive.
Case of a lifetime!
Nope you can't win them all
This is one you can beat,
To make your name stand tall.
This is the case that's going to put you all on your own.
No-one says you can win.
We don't listen to y'all.
Like Israel lost in the wilderness,
We just want to turn around
Keep believing God is the reason
Each time your foot hits the Ground.

THESE LETTERS SPEAK FOR ME

Locked in this cage, so the world can't hear me.
I meditate to the oracles, so that they can speak through me!
Talking to this world, that I Am not of.
My intercessor is the Holy Spirit! Who speaks with Jesus through love.
Thanks to Christ, I have a direct connection to Love.
My biggest concern is how do I teach this so that all can understand?
Truth given through love?
To get you my thoughts, I keep pens and pencils in mt hands!
My time will come to speak ,and it aint all about the paper.
Just wanting to get home! So I can raise my child
If you read any of my books, you can see my mood;
Flows up and down.
Follow my progression, while I imprint it upon the mind.
Got too much to teach these young boys and girls
Everything works for good in the kingdom of God.
You've been given the choice of free will
And the consciousness embedded in deep thought.
Engrained with a spirit to know wrong from right
Which side of your spirit will you listen?
Left brain? Or right? Top or bottom?
Does anyone's cerebral cortex think? Conscience to follow.
The Holy Bible hardly speaks of the Tree Of Life;
Those few are important knowledge
The Tree of Life near the river of life
Whose leaves were for the healing of the nations.
Re-read the book of revelations and look at what we're facing.
Trouble on the horizon so I hope you confess to Jesus
These letters speak from She
I talk what's God given.

I AM CALEB

Trudging through an unfamiliar land,
Looking for some water in all of this sand.
Wanting to turn around and head back to Egypt
Not enough faith to believe that God has the perfect plan;
To lead us, Passing on through these difficulties
On the way to a land flowing with milk and honey:
Upon our arrival, we fear its inhabitants
When God's already in front of us.
Among the masses, there's only one Caleb;
Blessed with a different spirit.
Willing to give up this life for thee.
Put it all down for the chance to follow thee.
How many of us are true heroes? Willing to fight like She?
Thank you lord for leading our steps:
Signed Caleb, Jesus and now me.

WHO WILL REPRESENT US

From the oval office to the board room
Where will you find me now?
From the senate panel to the decision panel
We still playing hide and seek at the trial.
The most presented face in the courtroom,
But the least represented seems to be.
I'm facing years in the penitentiary,
Never even said I did it.
Just received a story,
And you drew the logical conclusion onto who is guilty.
In the world that God rules,
Human logic is not what rules it.
Look into the unseen, and there you will find the truth in it.
What you tell me is impossible;
That is exactly what I will do.
Thank you Hugh Clarke for having faith in me
God sent you to do battle for broken youth!
When my enemies wanted to bury me;
Who will you train to be the next in likeness to you?
Your expertise is needed in Lansing, MI and across the world too.
Without you what will we do?
So many scared to stand up and make waves in this system,
Stuck in between a fight that must be.
How many more are out there just like me?
How many innocent souls are where they don't need to be?
By the tainted vote of our society
You tell me all is fair in love and war,
Even America put sanctions on how guerilla
The warfare in Iraq could go.
So their soldiers dropping arms
Hands up,
But still you shoot at me.
Attempt to take my life away,
And I was the State Police. Fire me without a
Trial, but I love the heat.
When God makes me big in life, I'll call you
To represent me.

ONLY IF YOU KNOW ME

Paint me out to be a criminal, a dangerous mind!
You couldn't even make me crazy,
When you forced me to do all of this time.
Kept faith in God; Belief set that She knows the way
Instead of looking to the stars,
Took trips to the depths of me each and every day.
Now here I stand
A man of Ausar; Understand?
Not in amount but in likeness onto them,
I am the power of God that lives deep within me.
Took my spirituality on a quest.
He finds strength,
Especially in my weaknesses.
Go ahead and keep listening to the papers.
Believing that this is the final outcome of me.
I apologize. I tripped into this,
Up into a broken prison system for all to see.
God is the only true witness for me.

I AM THE YOUNG SON

I am the young son who asked God my portion,
And it was given onto me:
Watch me journey to a far country, and waste away
Mine own possessions.
Now the famine is here, and this country will give me nothing.
Knowing my father is rich, I swallow my pride and return home.

Pre-planning what to say to him once I do finally make it home.
Though I was still far away,
My Father noticed me
He had compassion though I knew I was wrong.
He happily ran to meet me,
And embraced me, as if I was never gone.
I began to explain, and He only shushed away my shame.
Sent servants to get the best for me, welcomed me home again.
For my spirit was dead, now I Am alive again.
For I was lost; now I have been found by direction in this life.
Don't be mad older sister, I wish to be like you
You've always been right here with Father
I was the one all confused

OPTIMISM IS THE MOST IMPORTANT HUMAN TRAIT BECAUSE IT ALLOWS US TO EVOLVE OUR IDEAS, TO IMPROVE OUR SITUATION, AND TO HOPE FOR A BETTER TOMORROW.

SETH GODIN

ALL THAT WE ARE IS THE RESULT OF WHAT WE HAVE THOUGHT. THE MIND IS EVERYTHING. WE THINK, WE BECOME.

BUDDHA